THE ART OF THE PROGRAM

Matt Brittingham

The content of the Book, including but not limited to text, images, graphics, and illustrations, is protected by copyright and other intellectual property laws. All rights are reserved by the author and publisher, and no part of the Book may be reproduced, distributed, or transmitted in any form without prior written permission.

With great power comes great responsibility; reading this book might not give you superpowers but to mere mortals it may appear like you have become some type of digital wizard.

The Reader understands and agrees that they are using the Book at their own risk. The author and publisher shall not be held liable for any direct or indirect damages, including but not limited to personal injury, financial loss, or any other harm resulting from the use of the Book or reliance on its content.

The content provided in the Book is for informational and educational purposes only. It is not intended to serve as legal, financial, medical, or any other professional advice - it's a highly opinionated text based on years of experience. Also, I'm not starting a cult but have considered it. Use of the guidelines in this book is a choice of the reader.

While the author and publisher have made every effort to ensure the accuracy and reliability of the information contained in the Book, they do not guarantee its completeness or correctness. The content may become outdated or subject to errors, and the author and publisher disclaim any liability for any inaccuracies or omissions that may occur.

The Book may contain links to external websites or resources. These links are provided for convenience and do not signify endorsement by the author or publisher of the linked content. The author and publisher have no control over external sites and cannot be held responsible for their content, privacy policies, or practices. Readers should exercise caution when visiting external links.

The Reader assumes full responsibility for their interpretation and use of the information presented in the Book. They should exercise discretion and judgment when applying any ideas or concepts contained therein.

The author and publisher reserve the right to modify or update this disclaimer at any time without prior notice.

By proceeding with the Book, the Reader acknowledges that they have read and understood this disclaimer and agree to its terms. If the Reader does not agree with any part of this disclaimer, they should discontinue the use of the Book immediately.

This disclaimer is governed by the laws of jungle, and any disputes arising from its use shall be subject to the exclusive jurisdiction of the courts in galactic federation of Plan 9 from Outer Space.

DEDICATION

This book is dedicated to all the real ones out there...
the ones that want to make a dent in the universe.

Table of Contents

Table of Contents

Table of Contents

Table of Contents

Introduction

Whether this is your first time attempting to learn how to program or you've been dipping your toes into programming for a little bit, this book will help you to understand "how to program".

I'm going to hold your hand and lead you in the way that I would have wanted to be led into the world of programming.

I'm going to be the mentor for you, that I never had.
…

One of the biggest challenges with programming is actually not in writing the code or memorizing syntax, it's actually in learning how to think.

Have you ever really thought about what thinking is?

We all think, however, when you really "think" about it, there is a lot more going on beneath the surface of what "thinking" actually is.

Stay with me, because you need to understand what I'm really saying, when I say, "learning how to think".
…

Thinking programmatically or "thinking like a programmer" is basically like writing a recipe.

Some recipes are simple, for example: "Here's 3 ingredients, throw this in the fridge overnight and it's done."

Then there's other recipes that have tons of exotic ingredients, phases and steps to them.

A great example is sushi, to actually make good sticky rice takes so much prep work! You need to rinse all the starch off it, you have to cook it and add vinegar and keep turning it, you can't let it burn, etc. The point is, it's a long complex process.

The number one thing that I see people new to programming get stuck on is this "thinking" ability... Some pick it up faster than others.

With the right mental framework, this way of thinking will naturally start to become easier for you. Eventually, it just becomes instinctual - a natural, default way that you think when you sit down to write code.

You will know that you've really integrated this way of thinking when you start doing it outside of programming. You'll just start seeing problems and breaking them down into smaller parts, and then those parts, into steps.

Eventually, it just becomes effortless, you don't even have to think about it.

Why I wrote this book

I'm new to content creation and I have been posting videos on TikTok trying to understand how social media works and how video content works. Long story short, I posted a video about the Raspberry Pi and how I thought it was pretty much the most important thing I ever bought that helped me learn to program. The video got more responses than any of my other videos. A lot of people had a lot of different questions.

The questions would be things like what were two to three books that you use to learn Linux and how to use the Raspberry Pi. There were also questions that were, in a sense, very beginner focused, like someone's first exposure to seeing the Raspberry Pi and not understanding what it was, how to use it, or why they would even want to. I made a few response videos to some comments explaining things to people and they seemed to appreciate that. Fast forward to a month later and I was still getting more questions... so I decided that I would write a book to show people how I would learn if I was starting today. This is the book that I would have wanted to have picked up as my first book.

The goal for this book is not to make you a "Jedi Master" of programming. The goal for this book is to get you prepared with just enough knowledge to be dangerous and to also give you the mindset and the mentality to be able to stand up on your own two feet so that you can keep moving forward. Give me your trust, follow along, and I'll show you the ropes.

High barrier to entry?

Before you can begin to write code, you will need to get your development environment set up.
It's a bit of a process, you're going to need to make some decisions, try some things out and then figure out what works best for you.

I'm using this term "development environment" very broadly because it can mean a lot of things to a lot of people. Basically, it's where you're going to work on your code. The decision you make on where and how you want to work is up to you. I'll be giving you some guidance and suggestions later on in the book.

Programming concepts expectations

There are probably only a dozen concepts you really need to memorize in order to get rolling with programming. A few of these are things like variables, loops, functions, and arrays. Don't worry about if the names seem confusing - it's computer science, believe me, this won't be the last time you scratch your head wondering about what something means.

That said, the basics are the basics. They're fundamental, they're foundational. You need to understand the first dozen or so of them with instant recall. It's not going to happen overnight, so just take your time and learn them.

I fear not the man who has practiced 10,000 kicks once, but I fear the man who has practiced one kick 10,000 times. - Bruce Lee

Demystifying A Programmer Myth

Most programmers don't know what they are doing. Yes, you read that correctly, and yes, I generalized here. Let me explain -

I've built apps in Django, which is a python library, essentially it helps you build websites. That said, for the past year, I've been primarily building apps in JavaScript. So, if you asked me today to go and make you a web app with Django, I would have to take some time to re-learn or refresh myself on Python and Django. I wouldn't be a total beginner though, because I already understand a lot of the fundamental concepts involved with building a website or a web app.

These would be things like how to talk to and get data from an API. How to query a database to change something or get something. Additionally, on the frontend, I could then display the results from the response.

That's all well and good, but I would also understand how to save my work and how to share my work with a friend or a teammate. I would also know what's involved with hosting a website, etc.

See what I'm getting at?

So, two things to keep in mind:
1. You won't be able to remember everything.
2. Learn the fundamentals because they will stick with you.

Reading documentation

Programming documentation can be confusing at first, it's going to be filled with different symbols that you're not going to be used to reading. It can seem overwhelming at first but after you read this type of writing for a while, you start to appreciate it.

It does take a bit of getting used to though, so take your time with it, and don't worry if it doesn't make sense for a while because it will eventually. The main point is don't get caught up about it, just figure out what you're trying to do and keep moving.

Ye Intruders Beware

Yes, that was a "Goonies" reference – I digress.

Introduction

Here's a little diagram that I made (I know, it's super simple). This diagram has 2 sides - left and right (good and bad). Being frustrated is a big part of programming, it's basically a never ending constant. If you stay frustrated for 2 hours or more, then you're going to increase your stress level. If you push yourself to hard by continuing to stress yourself out, then you're going to get overwhelmed and increase the likelihood of getting burned out.

One thing leads to another... Frustration -> stress -> overwhelm -> burnout

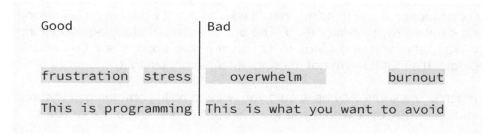

Overwhelm

If you find yourself getting overwhelmed, slow down, take a break or go get a glass of water and come back later. Most likely you've just tried to cram too much into your brain too fast. I get it, we all do it. A good programmer is always mindful of this. It's an instinct you will develop overtime. Rule of thumb here, don't spend more than 15 minutes breaking your brain on something. You spin your tires too long and you're gonna get stuck in the mud and it can ruin your day. Just take some breaks.

Burnout

What is burnout and what does it feel like? In the simplest terms possible, it means you're not going to be able to think. Your brain is going to feel like Jell-O or mush. You're basically done for the day, and in some cases, maybe a few days. You're not going to have the strength to really do anything, and it can lead to a downward spiral that will have the potential of really making your life difficult. So be aware of it.

Tinkering

Programming is super technical; it attracts technical people and technical people tend to tinker. You may find that, you too, have the propensity to tinker away with things to the point that you get bogged down in the weeds. While I get the allure of that, or why you may want to do that, I'm going to try to keep you "inside the rails" a little bit, at least that's the way that I approach programming.

You may think that you worked all day but in reality, you totally missed the boat because you were focusing too much on optimizing or fixing something that in the big picture of things, didn't really matter that much.

There's a time and a place for "Tinkering" - just make sure that you are dedicating a specific time for that. Hint: it's not when you're building.

Shiny Objects

Once you get into JavaScript and you've been programming for a little bit, you're going to see the hottest new library come out. Everyone is going to start posting on social media and making videos about it. You're probably going to find yourself thinking, "Oh my gosh this amazing shiny thing is amazing!". You may also think to yourself, "Wow, this is the shortcut I've been looking for!". You might even hear others proclaiming, "Oh my gosh you have to totally try this thing!", or "What are you even doing if you're not using this thing!".

My friend, these are what we call distractions...

Ignore them.

Personally, I tend to just acknowledge that something exists. Then during some downtime, some leisure time, maybe I'm watching something on Netflix or whatever. It's at this time that I'll take a look at what they're all talking about. I usually do this passively, checking it out on my phone or iPad. The point is, I'm not stopping everything I'm doing and then redirecting all of my time, attention and focus to something that sounds exciting and is promising to be the answer to all my problems. It's FOMO - I'm not missing out if I'm not using it.

Here's another way to think about it - It's much in the same way as; would you want to build something in Python, over would you want to build something in JavaScript, over would you want to build something in C# or Rails.

To the end user or the person actually using your program or your software, it's not really going to matter - they don't even care. So just pick something, stick with it, get comfortable with it, and then later on, if you want to experiment or explore in some other area, you will have the opportunity to. That's when you can scratch that itch.

Besides, when you adopt a new technology, especially something like a brand new technology, there's a pretty high likelihood that it might not be fully supported. For instance, it's not really compatible with a lot of things. It could be buggy, it might have vulnerabilities, it could lack support, the community is small or the documentation could be really bad or hardly exists at all, etc.

So for these reasons alone, I would say just stand off to the side and let the other nerds delve into it and geek out on it. Let them "Tinker" and figure it out. Give it some time but keep it on your radar - maybe 6 months to a year, then take a look at it when there's actually some stuff to look at. Otherwise, you're probably just wasting your time.

You just keep focusing - keep building things, keep making gains.

Getting stuck

It's going to happen. Let me break it down for you.

Programming is like playing the game "telephone" with a computer. You're literally taking some thought or idea in your head and translating it into text by typing on your keyboard. Your computer is then supposed to interpret and then do something with that.

So yeah, things are going to go wrong. What level the error occurs at; whether you misspelled something, misnamed a variable, had an error in logic, etc., is going to come down to your level of discernment with catching yourself.

Either way, you're going to have to get really good at catching your mistakes - this is a skill.

This is going to occur most often with new programmers who copy/paste code a lot. Don't do that. Actually read the code. Understand what the code is doing.

Learning how to ask for help

The holy grail for asking for help has to be without a doubt - Stack Overflow.

If you haven't heard about this site, it's pretty amazing. You can go to it directly at www.stackoverflow.com and that's cool, I know a lot of people do that. Usually, they're just looking around or want to see what different types of questions people are asking about.

However, the way that you're going to interact with Stack Overflow isn't by going directly to the website. Instead, you're going to go to Google. Then you're going to type into Google your question.

Here's an example:
type question into top bar

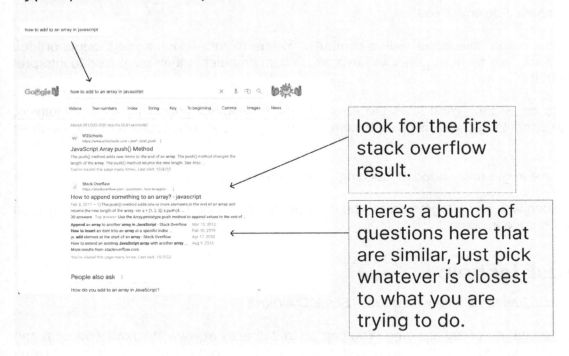

look for the first stack overflow result.

there's a bunch of questions here that are similar, just pick whatever is closest to what you are trying to do.

This is what I call "Google-Fu" - the best of the best programmers have good "Google-Fu".

How to ask a question correctly:

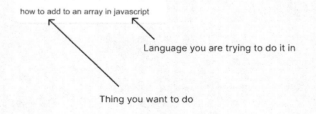

how to add to an array in javascript

Language you are trying to do it in

Thing you want to do

When you have a programming related question, you're going to type that into the Google search bar. The Google search is going to return you some results. You're then going to be looking for results from "Stack Overflow".

Ignore all the blogs or whatever else is out there, just stick to the "Stack Overflow" results because you're going to need to learn how to read them.

Using "Stack Overflow" this way is super important - it's going to expose you to seeing that not only do people solve problems differently, use different approaches, etc., but you also get to see how opinionated people are. You're going to see many different ways of solving things. One of the best things about this is how much it teaches you. You'll know you're improving when you catch yourself saying something like, "Okay, I was trying to solve it this way, but I never thought about solving it that way".

The Hack

I need to get this out of the way because it needs to be said. There is no hack, there is no short-cut or quick fix when it comes to learning this stuff.

It's going to take time, like when you start eating healthier or when you first start going to the gym. You're not going to see any results or gains for a while, maybe in a few months if you're lucky. I know it sounds cliche' but "trust the process".

As someone who has lived their life mastering new things, I'm telling you from experience, no one will notice, then everyone (including yourself) will.

Don't copy pasta

The fact that something like "Stack Overflow" exists is simply amazing. However, if used incorrectly, it's just going to limit your potential.

"Copy pasta" is slang for "copy/paste" - it's something that you should never, ever, do.

The reason that you don't copy code is because, chances are, that you won't understand it. The goal is to understand.

If you just copy/paste a bunch of code and you get your program working, well, then it's kind of like having a black box. Sure, it works, but you don't know what's inside of it, you don't know WHY the code is working. All you know is that it works.

What happens when something breaks? Even worse, what happens when you have a stack of these "black boxes" and you don't know how any of them work?

Well, I guess when something breaks, you're kind of in trouble...

That's why you take the time - you read through and review 5 to10 different answers. Then you decide which answer you like the most. It's only then, at that point, that you develop your *own* solution and add it to your code.

You don't just flat out copy the code, you look at the answer, you understand it, you reference it, and then, you go implement that answer inside of your code base.

Pitfalls and Edge cases

In programming there are so many of these gotchas.

It is my opinion that these gotchas are probably the largest contributing factor as to why people who attempt to learn programming can't seem to make it past the initial phase - they fall out, they give up.

There's not any particular set of phases a programmer needs to go through, it's not like playing a video game where you finish level 1 and move onto level 2. It's actually not like that at all.

Most places you go, either online, in a classroom environment or in book format, will tell you to learn HTML, CSS, JavaScript, and so on (usually in that order). They tell you to learn these languages in some sort of progressive manner or order.

It is my contention, or rather, belief, that this is the wrong way to learn and was a major factor in my motivation to write this book.

At its root, programming or "learning to program" isn't about memorizing syntax or knowing data structures and algorithms. It's about empowering yourself to be an unstoppable creative force for problem solving.

There should be a "no factor" mentality when approaching problem solving.

Meaning, you should be able to look at a problem and have the ability to begin solving it without the guidance or oversight from a tutorial, teacher, book, video, etc.

The difference between a "good" and a "bad" programmer is this exact ability.

Overtime, you will begin to develop your own process or methods for how you approach problem solving. As you grow as a programmer, you will naturally begin to refine your process. It will take less time to solve things and you will have more and more confidence.

This is the "root" idea behind this book - this is why I know that these pages are worth more than their weight in gold.

Fitness

A good programmer is also aware of their personal health.

Programming can lead to a very sedentary lifestyle. In order to mitigate this, you should be doing cardio regularly along with lifting. Get outside, go to the gym, go on jogs and lift some heavy weight.

I'm a huge believer in taking the programming mindset and developing it out further outside of just writing code.

Aside from the physical benefits, getting outside for a jog or brisk walk will also help you to clear your mind. I can't tell you how many times I've been out on a run and suddenly figured out the solution to a coding problem I've been trying to solve.

Workstation

Introduction

What's a workstation? Your workstation is the place where you will be writing code. It's the computer that you will be working from to build and develop your software.

We're all in different situations so our access to resources is going to vary. Some of us may have less resources than others. Regardless, in order to have a workstation you really only need a few things:

computer (mac, pc, Linux)
Internet Connection
Text Editor
IDE
Web Browser

If you have these things, then you can code.

Whether you are installing Linux on a new machine, using your existing computer with its OS or setting up a Raspberry Pi. Taking these factors into consideration, getting your workstation setup should take around 1-2 hours MAX.

Here are a few methods of getting your workstation setup.

Overview

Starting from a blank slate is hard. You're going to have to make some decisions here.

A few questions to ask yourself are:

Do you set up your development environment/workspace on your current computer?
Do you buy a raspberry pi?
Do you get an older laptop to run Linux?

Don't get caught up in whether you should use this or that. Just make a decision and keep moving forward. Personally, I recommend trying all 3 approaches.

At the end of the day, it's about being able to quickly get set up so that you can start writing code as fast as possible. You just need a place to practice so that you can start building things.

Keep your focus on building something - that's the outcome.

Pros/Cons

Here's the cost/benefit/pros/cons of each decision:

Raspberry Pi
It's a clean state, you start with nothing.
If you break something, it's easy to get back to that clean slate again.
You will be using Linux; you will have to learn about the OS more.

Linux
It's a clean state, you start with nothing.
If you break something, it's easy to get back to that clean slate again.
You will be using Linux; you will have to learn about the OS more.

Mac
Not everyone has a mac.
You're working on your daily driver machine.

Windows
Not everyone has a PC.
You're working on your daily driver machine.
The command line is different.

Cheap laptops to buy

Google "amazon Best Sellers in Traditional Laptop Computers"

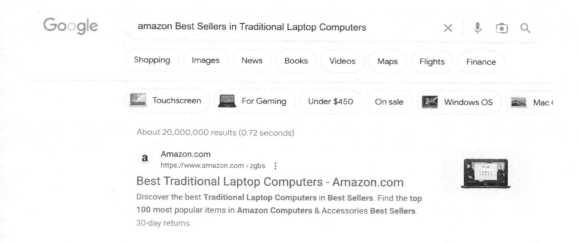

Here's what comes up when you click that link.

This is how much the laptop that I am using costs if you were to buy it off Amazon.

If you buy a laptop, try to get one that has at least an i5 or better processor with at least 4gb of ram and 128gb hard disk. Try to get one with an SSD drive, it will make your system run super-fast and snappy.

Step 3

Flash the ISO to the USB. Click the "Flash" button.

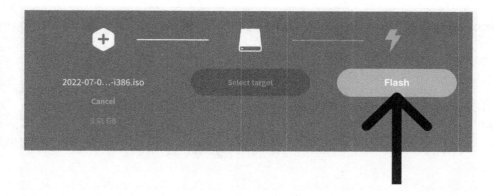

It's going to take a few minutes to burn the ISO. After it's finished, you should see a screen similar to this.

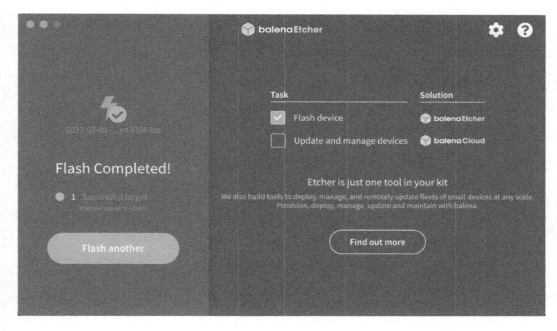

Unplug the USB from your machine and plug it into your workstation.

Workstation

Booting from USB

Intro

Prior to running the USB with your new operating system on your machine, you must instruct the computer to initiate booting from the USB.

To enable booting from the USB on your laptop, you should have the capability to access the boot menu.

The boot menu is a component of the BIOS (Basic Input/Output System) responsible for indicating the location of your operating system to the computer.

How to boot from USB

Before you can get the USB with your new OS to run on your machine, you will first need to tell the computer to boot from the USB.

In order to boot from the USB on your laptop you will need to be able to access the boot menu.

A boot menu is part of the bios, it's what tells your computer where your OS is.

If you don't know how to boot your workstation from the USB, you have 2 options:

A. Google it
B. Go to disk-image.com

Google it Method

If you go the google route to look up how to boot from USB, you can just type something like this: "[computer model] boot menu". See Example.

disk-image.com Method

Go here: https://www.disk-image.com/faq-bootmenu.htm

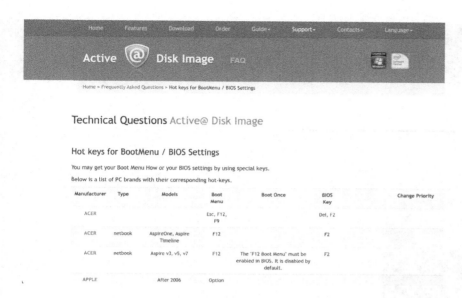

Home > Frequently Asked Questions > Hot keys for BootMenu / BIOS Settings

Technical Questions Active@ Disk Image

Hot keys for BootMenu / BIOS Settings

You may get your Boot Menu How or your BIOS settings by using special keys.

Below is a list of PC brands with their corresponding hot-keys.

Manufacturer	Type	Models	Boot Menu	Boot Once	BIOS Key	Change Priority
ACER			Esc, F12, F9		Del, F2	
ACER	netbook	AspireOne, Aspire Timeline	F12		F2	
ACER	netbook	Aspire v3, v5, v7	F12	The "F12 Boot Menu" must be enabled in BIOS. It is disabled by default.	F2	
APPLE		After 2006	Option			

Hitting ctrl + f type in the manufacturer of your laptop. It will show you the results for your laptop.

Lenovo makes the t420. It looks like f12 is the button to push to open the boot loader.

LENOVO	desktop		F12, F8, F10		F1, F2	
LENOVO	laptop		F12		F1, F2	
LENOVO	laptop	IdeaPad P500	F12 or Fn + F11		F2	

Installing Linux on your workstation

Put the USB into your laptop, turn your laptop on and start hitting the f12 button continuously until the boot menu opens.

Select boot from USB from the boot menu. Here's what it looks like on my laptop, the t420.

"USB HDD: USB DISK 2.0"

Workstation

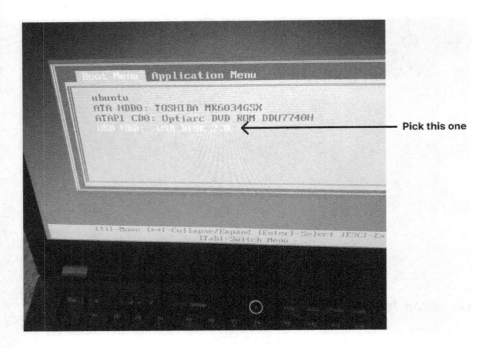

Pick this one

After reading the USB, it's going to ask you what you want to do.

Pick "Graphical install".

Pick this one ——→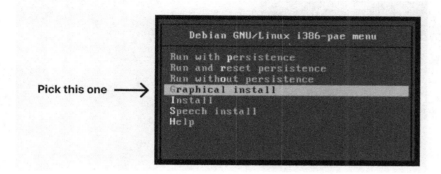

The graphical installer program should now load up for you.

Pick the keyboard type that you are using. For me, I picked - "American English".

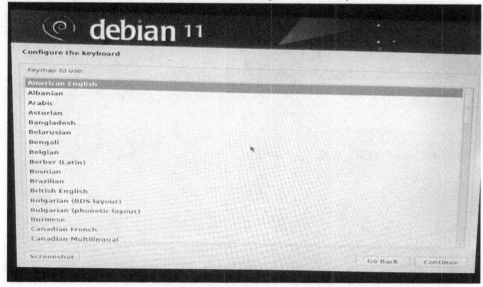

Next, you will see it install some additional components.

When the system reboots, you are going to see the GRUB screen. You don't need to do anything here; it will automatically load the OS for you after a few seconds.

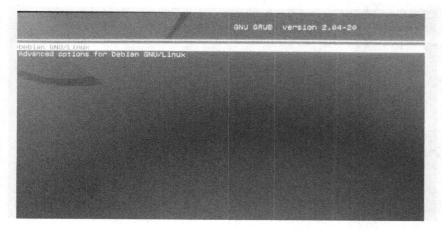

Booting Linux screen

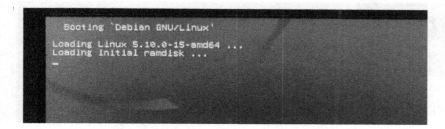

Splash screen

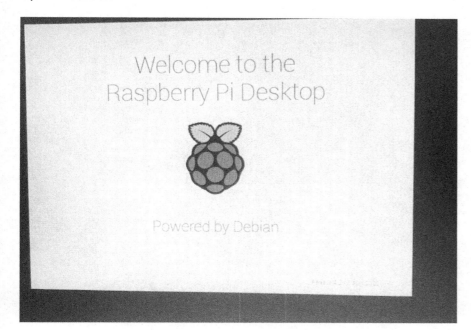

Workstation

You should now see your desktop.

Official install tutorial by Raspberry Pi Foundation

If you encounter any issues with your installation, you can go here to view the official install guide.
https://projects.raspberrypi.org/en/projects/install-raspberry-pi-desktop/0

Setting up your workstation

The OS you are using is called "Raspbian".

There's a ton of helpful documentation here to help you with moving around and using your new OS.
https://www.raspberrypi.com/documentation/computers/os.html

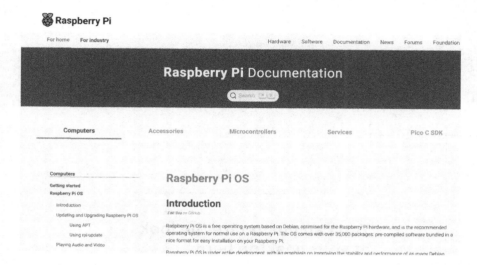

To keep things simple, here's a quick overview of how to navigate around.

Task bar

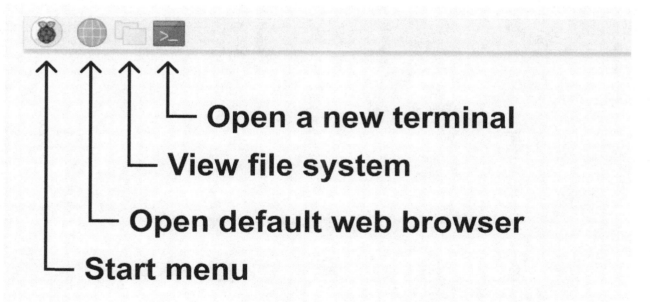

Open a new terminal

View file system

Open default web browser

Start menu

Workstation

Customizing Your Desktop

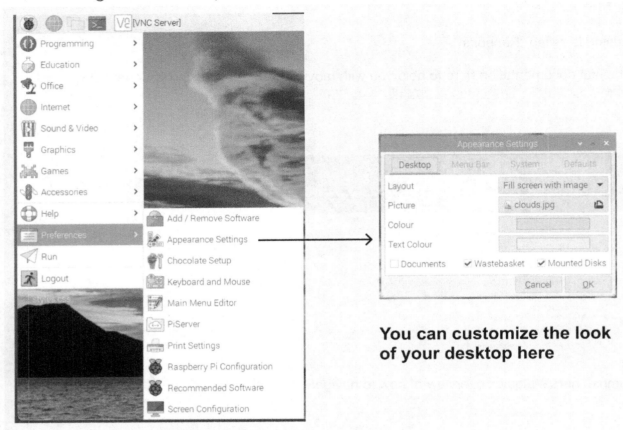

You can customize the look of your desktop here

Create a Projects Folder

We're going to be working on a few projects in this book.

Go ahead and create a projects folder on your desktop, this will make it much easier to follow along in the exercises when we do them.Right-click anywhere on your desktop and select "New Folder".

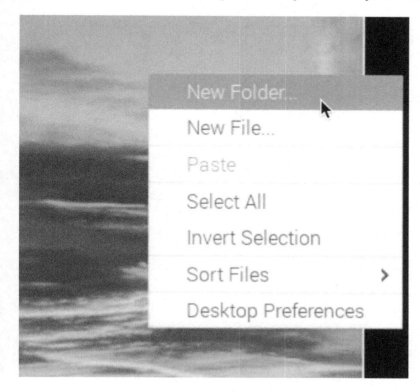

Next, name the folder "PROJECTS".

*I made the name of the folder all CAPS.

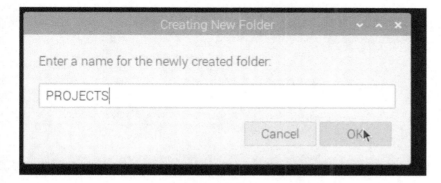

As you can see, Linux isn't really that different from Mac or Windows (at least when it comes to using a desktop). A lot of the same things that you're used to with these other platforms are the same here. The way that you make a new folder on your desktop is basically the same.

We don't need to do anything else with this folder right now, so let's move on to the next topic.

Linux 101

The version of Linux I'm going to recommend that you use is **Raspbian**.

Raspbian is a Linux operating system based on the Debian Linux distribution that was developed for the Raspberry Pi.

Uh. what?

Linux is an operating system.

Debian is a version of Linux (a distribution).

To really oversimplify it, Linux is just like MacOS or Windows - it's an operating system.

People often call Linux distribution's - distros.

There's 100's of different distributions, some people can really nerd out on them.

You can literally customize every aspect of your OS. Don't believe me? Type "linux distro reddit" into google and check out all the active subreddits.

Basically...

A Linux distribution is a Linux kernel, GNU tools and libraries, software, programs, documentation, a window system (X Window System / Wayland), a window manager, desktop environment and some sort of package manager.

BTW - "GNU" is pronounced "guh-new".

If you want to learn more about this google "richard stallman gnu linux" - this man is a national treasure.

Man Pages

If I don't mention this I'm going to catch a lot of shade from the neckbeards.

Short for manual pages, this is the OG way people would look up different flags for commands. It's worth checking out.

If you have a terminal open, you can just type man at the command line like this.

```
matt@raspberry:~ $ man
What manual page do you want?
For example, try 'man man'.
matt@raspberry:~ $ ▮
```

Ah, it looks like the man pages have their own man page - how meta.

Now type, man man.

```
matt@raspberry:~ $ man man▮
```

You should now see the man page for the man command.

```
MAN(1)                       Manual pager utils                       MAN(1)

NAME
       man - an interface to the system reference manuals

SYNOPSIS
       man [man options] [[section] page ...] ...
       man -k [apropos options] regexp ...
       man -K [man options] [section] term ...
       man -f [whatis options] page ...
       man -l [man options] file ...
       man -w|-W [man options] page ...

DESCRIPTION
       man  is  the  system's manual pager.  Each page argument given to man is
       normally the name of a program, utility or function.  The  manual  page
       associated with each of these arguments is then found and displayed.  A
       section, if provided, will direct man to look only in that  section  of
       the  manual.   The  default action is to search in all of the available
       sections following a pre-defined order (see DEFAULTS), and to show only
       the first page found, even if page exists in several sections.

       The table below shows the section numbers of the manual followed by the
Manual page man(1) line 1 (press h for help or q to quit)
```

These "man pages" can be pretty long. To read through them you can either scroll with your mouse, use the arrow keys or the PgUp/PgDn keys.

To exit the man pages, press "q".

Let's check out what `ls` means

```
matt@raspberry:~ $ man
What manual page do you want?
For example, try 'man man'.
matt@raspberry:~ $ man man
matt@raspberry:~ $ man ls
```

This is the man page for the `ls` command.

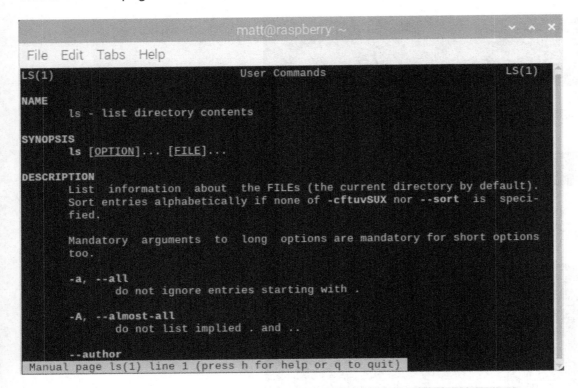

To recap, type: `man <whatever command you want to know about>`

Personally, I rarely use man pages, we live in the age of Google. If I need to learn about something I usually just google it and spend 5 minutes learning about it that way.

Alas, for historical purposes and street cred, knowing this exists is probably worth it.

It's all files

One of the biggest breakthroughs for me was realizing that linux is nothing more than a bunch of text files. You edit these text files and your computer changes the way it works.

For example, when you go to your settings or preferences menu on your computer and click "adjust volume" or "change mouse cursor direction" this is all just a GUI layer that sits on top of the system's program files. It abstracts away the files that you would need to edit and handles all of that for you via you interacting with the GUI (graphical user interface).

When you start editing these files yourself, it's really an "ah-ha" moment. Kind of like how you can drive stick (manual transmission) vs. automatic in your car.

File System & File Permissions

The Linux filesystem is a thing all its own.

The way a file system is set up on one machine can differ from another but the basics of "why" and "how" it works remain the same.

In this book, we're just going to be working within our home directory (it's the place that our personal files are stored).

Everything in Linux is represented through the file system. This includes things like:
- Data (your files)
- Devices (keyboard, mouse, hard drive, wifi, etc.)
- Directories (your home folder, etc.)

That said, you shouldn't run into any instances with this book where you need to understand the file system or permissions.

However, if you want to learn more about the file system and permissions then my suggestion would be to do a search for "linux file system" on YouTube. I would avoid learning through blog posts at the beginner stage because they can be overly complex. Just watch a few videos from a few different people on YouTube and you should be able to pick it up.

BASH

Make your first BASH script

Open your projects directory on your desktop.

Create a new folder inside that directory called "bash_scripts". After you create the folder, go ahead and close the window.

Next, open a new terminal then type the following:
```
$ cd Desktop/PROJECTS/bash_scripts/
```

```
matt@raspberry:~ $ cd Desktop/PROJECTS/bash_scripts/
matt@raspberry:~/Desktop/PROJECTS/bash_scripts $ 
```

Create a new file called "my_first_bash_script.sh"
```
$ touch my_first_bash_script.sh
```

Confirm that the file was created.
```
$ ls
```

```
matt@raspberry:~/Desktop/PROJECTS/bash_scripts $ ls
my_first_bash_script.sh
```

Open the file in nano:
```
$ nano my_first_bash_script.sh
```

Then, type the following into nano:

```
#!/usr/bin/env bash
echo "hello world!";
echo "this is my first bash script!"
# This is a comment
```

Here's how mine looks

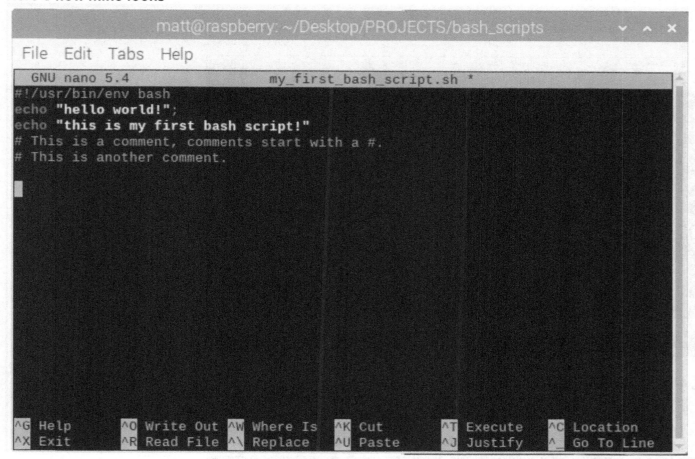

The first line contains the "Shebang" (#!/usr/bin/env bash). This first line specifies the script interpreter that's used to execute this script - i.e., BASH. The takeaway here is that if you don't have this shebang at the top of your script then your machine isn't going to know what shell to run the script in. You don't have to know what all this means yet, but you do need to know that you need it in order to run scripts.

The echo commands on lines 2 and 3 just means "print this to the console".

Comments start with a hash (#), comments aren't executed, they are there for us to take notes.

Press CTRL + O to save your file.

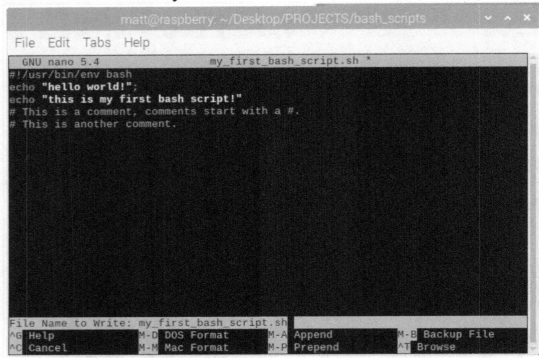

Press Enter to complete saving your file.

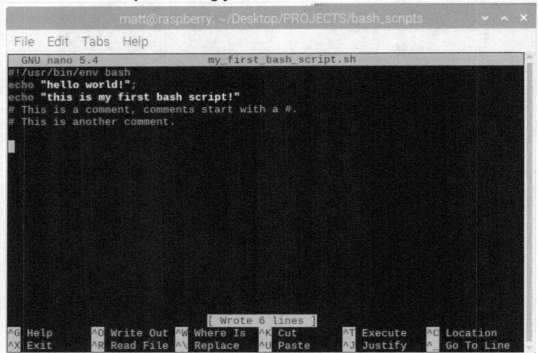

Then press CTRL + X to exit Nano.

P.s. If you hit CTRL + X to exit Nano before saving, it will pop up this message. You can still save here, just hit "y".

```
Save modified buffer?
 Y  Yes
 N  No                ^C  Cancel
```

View the contents of your file

Let's verify that the changes that we just made are actually in the file now.

Use the "cat" command to print the contents of your script file to the console (terminal).

```
matt@raspberry:~/Desktop/PROJECTS/bash_scripts $ cat my_first_bash_script.sh
#!/usr/bin/env bash
echo "hello world!";
echo "this is my first bash script!"
# This is a comment, comments start with a #.
# This is another comment.

matt@raspberry:~/Desktop/PROJECTS/bash_scripts $
```

Run a bash script from the shell

```
$ bash my_first_bash_script.sh
```

```
matt@raspberry:~/Desktop/PROJECTS/bash_scripts $ bash my_first_bash_script.sh
hello world!
this is my first bash script!
matt@raspberry:~/Desktop/PROJECTS/bash_scripts $
```

You can run bash scripts outside of the current directory as well but you first have to locate that file.

Here's what it looks like when I run the bash script from a new terminal window.

```
                          matt@raspberry: ~                    v  ^  x
 File  Edit  Tabs  Help
matt@raspberry:~ $ bash Desktop/PROJECTS/bash_scripts/my_first_bash_script.sh
hello world!
this is my first bash script!
matt@raspberry:~ $
```

In case you are wondering, "no, I did not remember the absolute path or location to the file". I used "tab completion".

I typed bash, then I typed capital "D". I then pressed TAB. After that I pressed Capital "P", then I pressed TAB again. Then "b", then TAB again, then "my", and then TAB again. After that, I just hit enter and it ran the script.

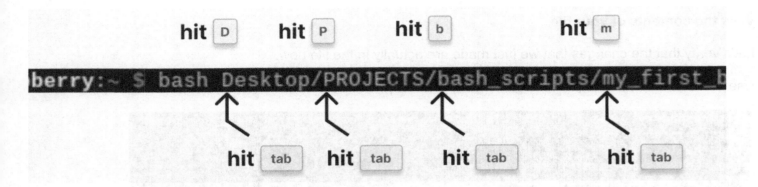

It seems complicated when you read it out like that. After a few minutes of moving around a file system, you'll get a handle on it and it'll become second nature.

Using both "ls" and "tab completion" is pretty much *essential* when you are navigating around a file system with a terminal. Just something to keep in mind because it's going to make your life a lot easier.

Unix based OSes are pretty cool in that way, they've thought of almost everything. I mean, they kind of had to. Desktop GUI's weren't a thing back in the day.

There's also additional options when using "ls", a lot of the time you will hear people refer to them as using different "flags". Instead of just typing "ls", try adding some flags like "ls -lh". There's even a help flag, "ls --help", it will show you a list of all the different flags you can try out.

Wrap up

Congrats, you just wrote your first bash script ;)

Scripting is a great way to get started with programming.

One of the coolest aspects about scripting is that it enables you to create automations for your computer. You might not see a need for it right now but it's something to be aware of because in the future there may come a time when you need to automate something.

This is a great site to reference the syntax for bash scripting: https://learnxinyminutes.com/docs/bash/

Command Line cheat sheet

Navigating the command line

Tab	autocomplete but for the terminal
Ctrl+C	exit the program
Ctrl+A	move cursor to beginning of line (a is first letter of alphabet)
Ctrl+E	move cursor to end of line (e stands for end)
Up/down arrow	review previous commands from history
left/right arrow	like tab for autocomplete

Common commands

cat	cat <filename>
nano	nano <filename>
ls	list files

Text Editors / IDE

Get acquainted with using a text editor and using an IDE.

There's a ton of different text editors and integrated development environments (IDE's) to pick from.

The main thing with text editors is that they're fast and lightweight. They load super-fast, and you can always keep one open and running in the background if you want to.

However, there's only one IDE that you should be using at this point and that's VS CODE. You will use them both often, sometimes even at the same time.

That said, you really only use VS CODE when you are writing code, it's an integrated development environment (IDE). VS Code is kind of heavy (it uses a lot more of your computer's resources). It's a very robust, full featured, customizable and expandable IDE. Basically, all that means is that it helps you out A LOT with writing code - you'll see what I mean later on.

To recap, for quick edits, note taking or just viewing some plain text, fast. A simple text editor is going to be your go to. If you're going to be working on a project or existing codebase filled with all kinds of files, use VS Code.

Text Editor

This is how you open the text editor. It comes pre-installed.

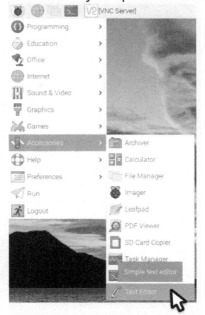

Text Editors / IDE

VS CODE
Visual studio code

If you are on your regular machine you can go to the vscode website to download and install vscode.

Installing VS CODE
If you are on the Raspberry Pi or using Linux follow these instructions:

OPEN TERMINAL AND PASTE

```
$ sudo apt update
$ sudo apt install code
```

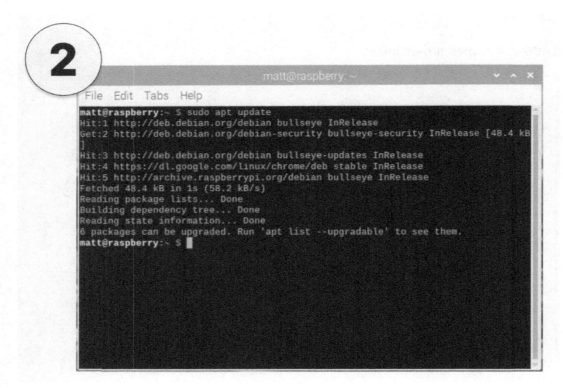

Let it run and update the packages

Install VS Code

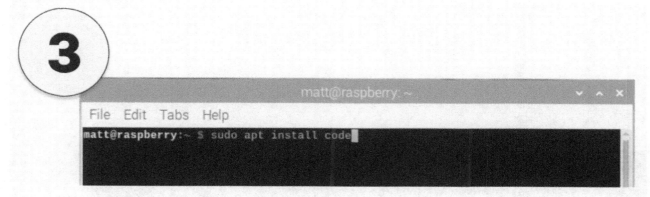

It's going to take a few minutes to install and download

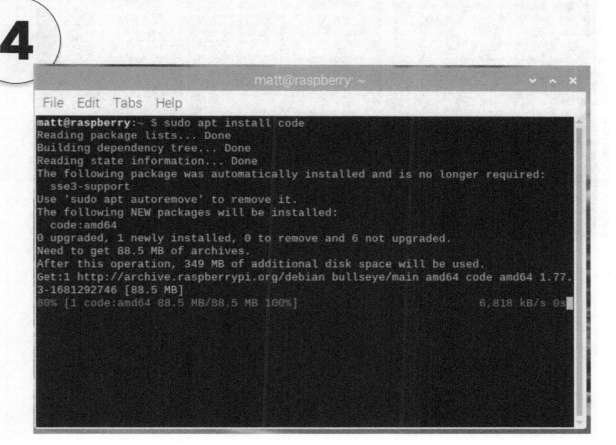

You should see this progress bar at some point

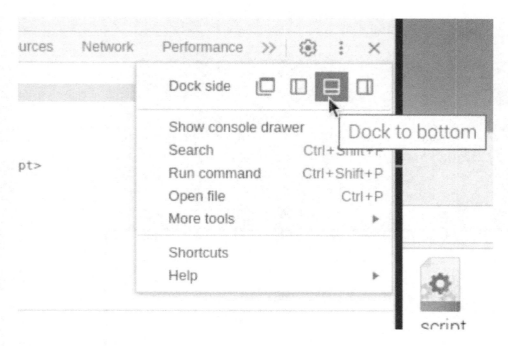

Basic devtools view

Text Editors / IDE

Focus on this bottom part

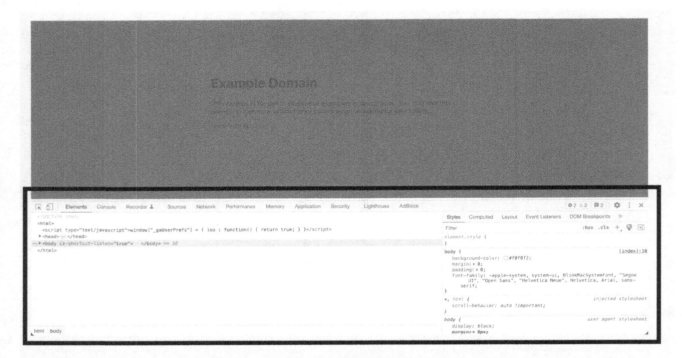

Pay attention to this part

These tabs are how you will navigate inside devtools.

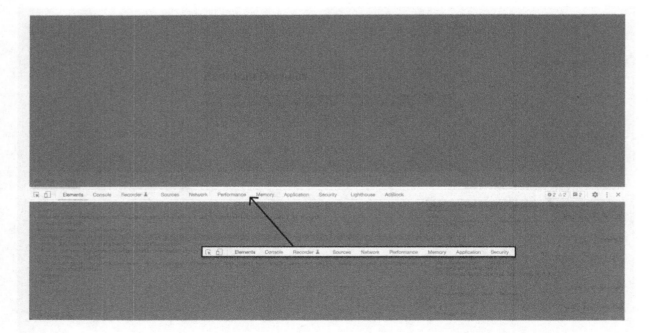

96

Navigating through your options in devtools

There are a few tabs at the top, if you click on one of these tabs you will see that it will have its own set of options. Each tab does something different. To keep things simple, we're just going to cover the first two tabs. You can google "how to use chrome dev tools" if you're interested in learning more than what I cover here.

For now, we're just going to focus on how to use these two tabs - "Elements" and "Console".

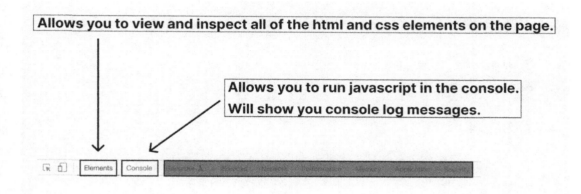

Allows you to view and inspect all of the html and css elements on the page.

Allows you to run javascript in the console.
Will show you console log messages.

*Console log messages are great for debugging your JavaScript code.

Ok, now that you know how to open devtools, let's experiment and learn how to use it.

Open devtools at www.example.com

Viewing Raw HTML

When viewing the raw HTML, you'll notice that when you move your mouse over the different tags/elements, that it will highlight the tag and the corresponding element on the page.

If you click the tag, it will "open up" (expand) and show you what's inside. We can drill down and view all the different parts of the page here.

Click on the body tag

When you move over the different elements, it will highlight them.

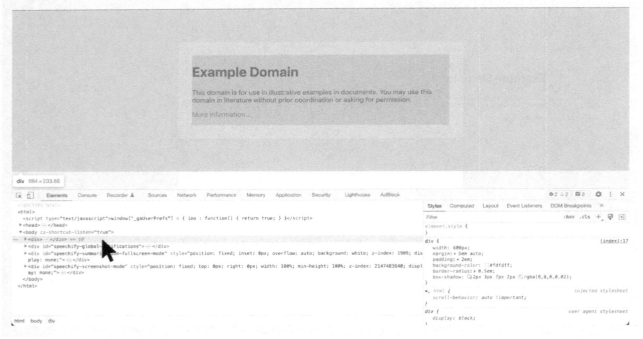

Highlighted h1 tag

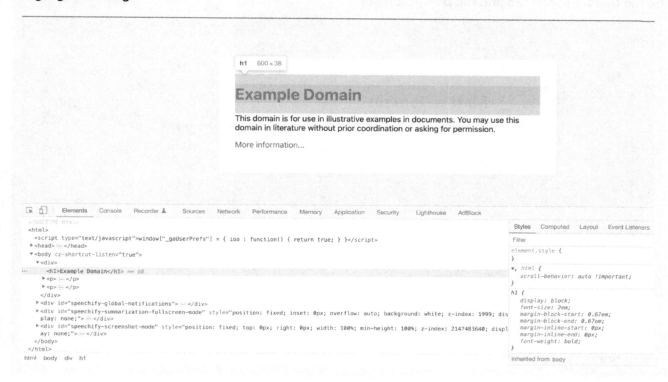

Double-clicked on the text in the highlighted h1 tag

```
<!DOCTYPE html>
<html>
  <script type="text/javascript">window["_gaUserPrefs"] = { ioo : function() { return true; } }</script>
  ▶<head> ⋯ </head>
  ▼<body cz-shortcut-listen="true">
    ▼<div>
⋯      <h1>Example Domain</h1> == $0
      ▶<p> ⋯ </p>
      ▶<p> ⋯ </p>
      </div>
    ▶<div id="speechify-global-notifications"> ⋯ </div>
    ▶<div id="speechify-summarization-fullscreen-mode" style="position: fixed; inset: 0px; overflow: auto; background: white; z-index: 1999; dis
      play: none;"> ⋯ </div>
    ▶<div id="speechify-screenshot-mode" style="position: fixed; top: 0px; right: 0px; width: 100%; min-height: 100%; z-index: 2147483640; displ
      ay: none;"> ⋯ </div>
    </body>
  </html>
html   body   div   h1
```

Paste the code that you just copied, into the text editor.

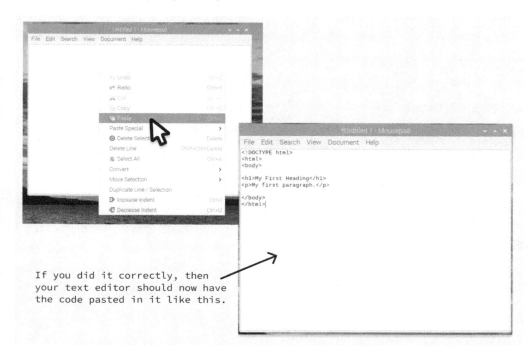

If you did it correctly, then your text editor should now have the code pasted in it like this.

To paste the code, right click in the text editor then click "Paste".

Once you paste the code in there, change the text inside of the <h1> tags from this to this:

`<h1>My First Heading</h1>`

`<h1>Hello World!</h1>`

Then change the text inside the <p></p> tags:

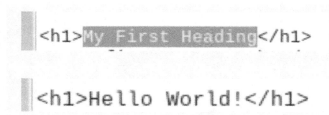

`<p>My first paragraph blah blah blah.</p>`

You can see I just added "blah blah blah".

Making your first web page

The final result should look something like this.

```
<!DOCTYPE html>
<html>
<body>

<h1>Hello World!</h1>
<p>My first paragraph blah blah blah.</p>

</body>
</html>
```

Next, in the text editor menu bar click, File > Save

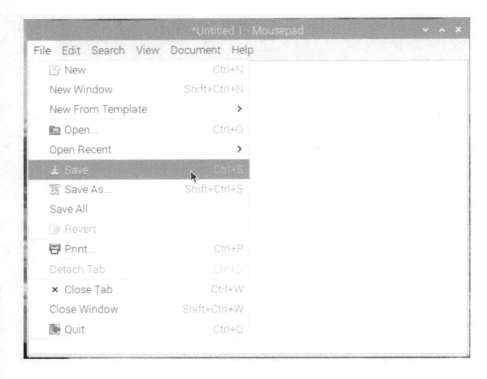

A new window should open up, give it the filename, "my_first_website.html", then save it to your desktop.

Notice, we are using the filename extension ".html" not ".txt", the reason for this is because we are making a webpage. In order for a web browser to read the code in the file, it needs the correct file extension (it needs to be an HTML file not a text file).

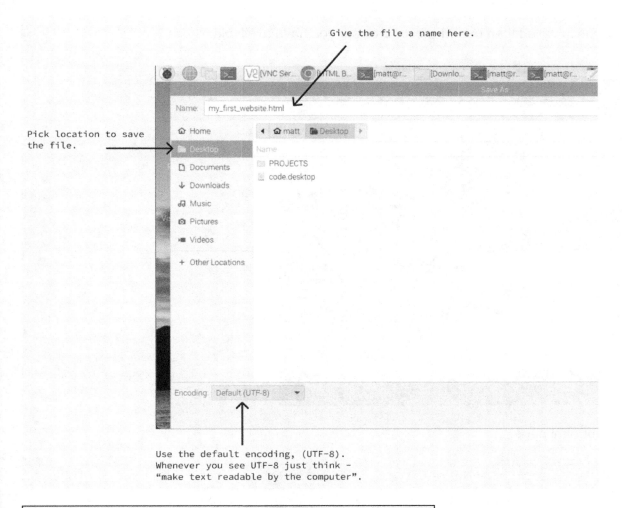

Give the file a name here.

Pick location to save the file.

Use the default encoding, (UTF-8). Whenever you see UTF-8 just think – "make text readable by the computer".

Sidenote - You may have noticed that I didn't add any spaces in my file name. This is because file systems don't work well with spaces. AVOID SPACES AT ALL COSTS. Instead use "hyphens" like, "**some-filename.txt**" or "underscores" like, "**some_filename.txt**". Trust me, just don't use spaces.

Making your first web page

Viewing our web page

Now if you go to your desktop, you should see the file.
Right click on it and then click "Open with > Google Chrome".

*If you don't have Chrome installed then use whatever browser you have available.

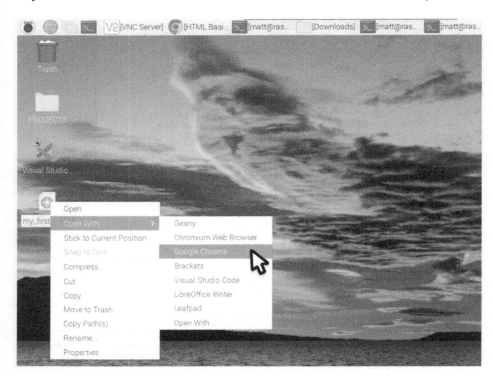

You should now see your html page.

The web browser shows you the file location of the .html file that you are viewing.

For giggles, I'm going to quickly change the file extension to .txt to show you how the browser interprets the code if it's a text file (.txt). You don't have to do this but I wanted you to see why using the correct file extension is important.

Here's how it should look in your code editor. Hit refresh on your browser after you have saved your stylesheet and you should see that the page background color has changed.

Step 3 - Basic JavaScript

Create a new file

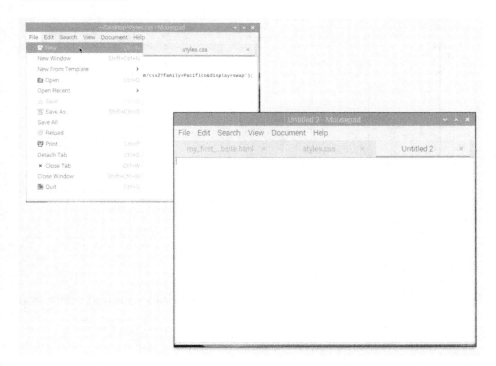

Making your first web page

Name the new file "script.js"

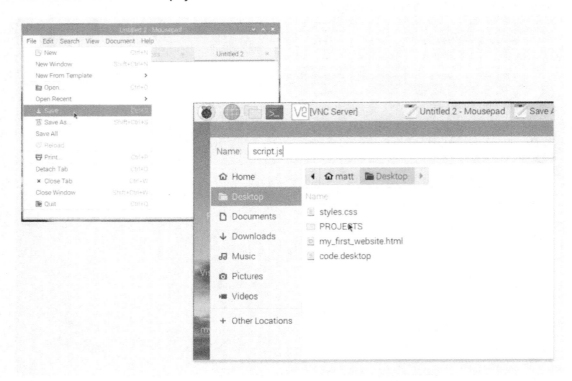

You should see the new file in your text editor now.

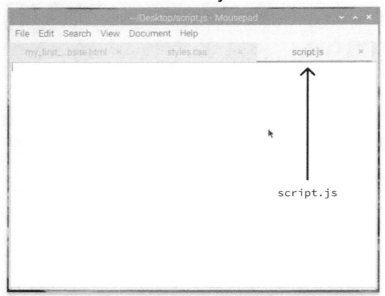

script.js

We're going to create an alert when you first view the webpage. Type the following code into your text editor and then hit save.

```
alert("I am an alert box!");
```

It should look like this

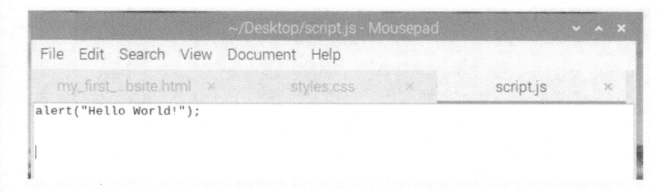

If you open your web page in the browser again you won't see anything. This is because we need to add the script to our web page.

Go ahead and open your "my_first_website.html" file.

Add this line of code:

```
<script src="script.js"></script>
```

It should look like this

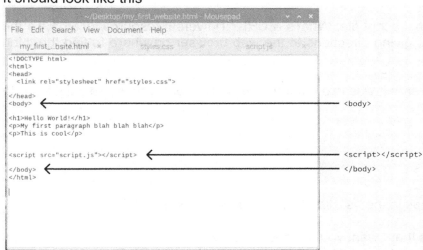

By including the script into our HTML like this, we have told our web page that when the browser loads, we need to pull in this script and run it.

Go ahead and open your page now.

Making your first web page

If you have done this correctly you will see this alert pop up.

How did this work? The script tag <script>, has an attribute called src.

```
<script src="script.js"></script>
```

The src attribute specifies the URL of an external script file. What's a URL? Universal resource locator, it's the path to the thing you want to use. Basically, it's giving directions to the web browser on where to find the thing that you are telling it to find.

In this case it was in the same directory. However, if it was in a different file or directory, you would tell it to go to that directory and then tell it which file to look for.

For example, a lot of times it would look like this:

```
<script src="js/script.js"></script>
```

So, your HTML file would tell the browser, go look in the "js" directory for the "script.js" file.

We'll get more into this later on, the main things that I want you to understand are:
- How an HTML file can have different dependencies (things it needs to run).
- How to include a stylesheet and JavaScript in your HTML.
- How a web browser finds those dependencies.

Step 4 - Basic File Structure

Close your text editor.

```
<!DOCTYPE html>
<html>
<head>
  <link rel="stylesheet" href="styles.css">

</head>
<body>

<h1>Hello World!</h1>
<p>My first paragraph blah blah blah</p>
<p>This is cool</p>


<script src="script.js"></script>

</body>
</html>
```

Right click on your desktop and create a new folder.

CSS Side quest

Intro

CSS was difficult for me to learn when I initially was starting out.

Aside from learning the basic syntax, it has a lot of weird rules and the way that you reference things can be a little confusing.

Take some time to review the resources below, then play around in your own local environment.

Resources

W3schools

https://www.w3schools.com

W3schools > CSS > go to "CSS Examples"

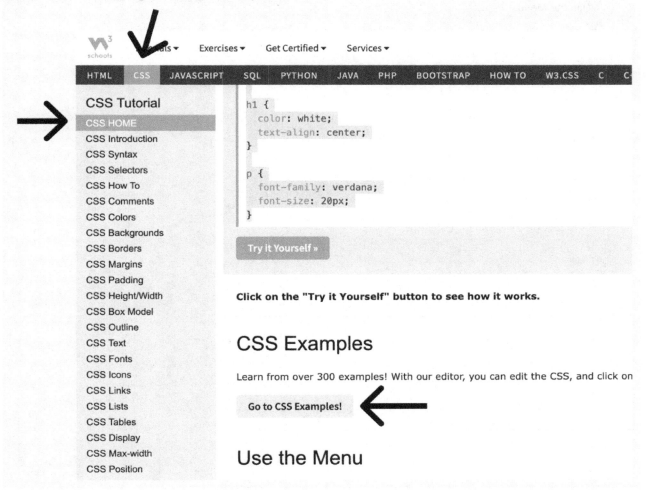

Intermission

This is a quick reference guide that you can search to help you find out how to do something quickly. Referencing a guide like this is going to make picking up CSS a lot easier for you.

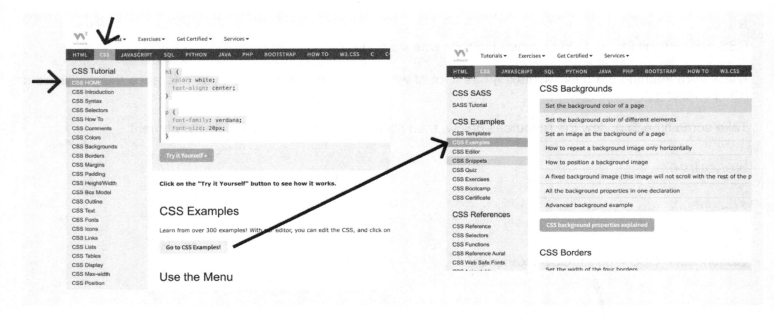

CodePen

CodePen is an amazing resource to learn about the true power of what's possible with CSS. It will give you the opportunity to see and understand how to use it from an expert level perspective.

There are TONS of examples here that you can hack on and play with to see the crazy things people are able to do with CSS.

I highly recommend that you check this site out.

https://codepen.io

Search results page

Type in a search term here

Intermission

Editor page (where you view the persons project or "pen")

edit html here　　　**edit css here**

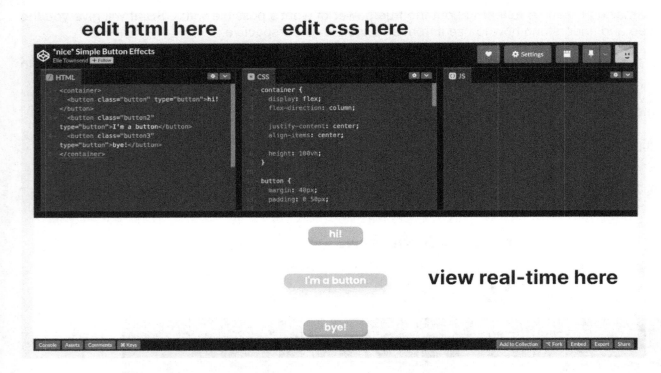

view real-time here

Project

Make a new folder in your projects folder and name it "learning_css".

In the folder create 2 files
- index.html
- styles.css

When that's done, copy this code in there.

HTML

```html
<!DOCTYPE html>
<html>
<head>
<link rel="stylesheet" href="styles.css">
</head>
<body>
<h2>Learning CSS</h2>
<button class="button">Button</button>
</body>
</html>
```

CSS

```css
body {
background-color: lightblue;
}
h1 {
color: white;
text-align: center;
}
p {
font-family: verdana;
font-size: 20px;
}

.button {
background-color: #4CAF50;
border: none;
color: white;
padding: 15px 32px;
text-align: center;
display: inline-block;
font-size: 16px;
margin: 4px 2px;
cursor: pointer;
}
```

Intermission

Here's how it should look:

Now that you have the basic page setup with your CSS, let's make a few changes to the button.

Try changing these things for your button:
- Change the height.
- Change the width.
- Change the font size.
- Change the color of the button.
- Give the button a shadow.
- Adjust the size of the shadow.

W3schools has a nice reference for how to style buttons on their site, so make sure to give that a look if you are struggling.

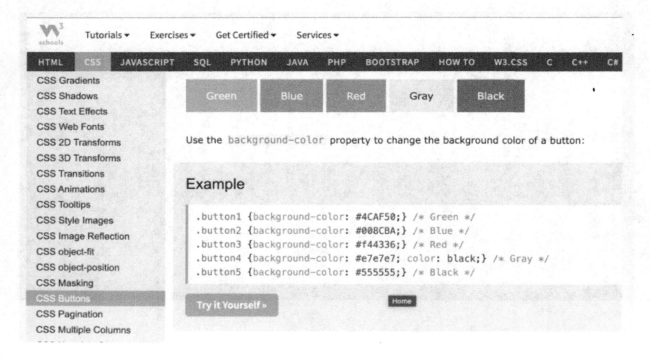

Layout

Next, let's work on the layout a bit. Try to make a box to put the button in. Then center the box and center the button inside of that box.

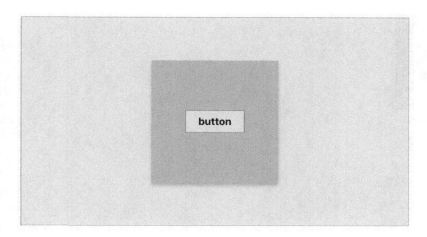

After that, make another box. This time in the second box, add a paragraph of text inside of it.

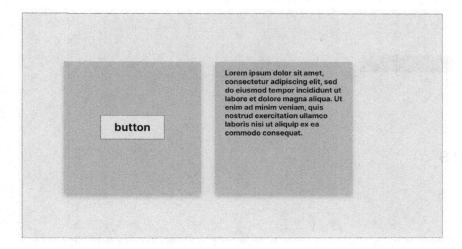

Intermission

Placeholder Text

You can grab some placeholder text from this site: https://loremipsum.io. It's a great site for placeholder text, so make sure to bookmark it and add it to your list of tools/resources.

At this point you should be referencing and getting a good understanding of selectors in CSS.

I'm going to give you my finished code to play around with. If you get stuck, look at my code, then add and remove different parts of the CSS. Deconstructing someone else's CSS code was the fastest way that I learned it.

From there, you will be dropped into the main screen.

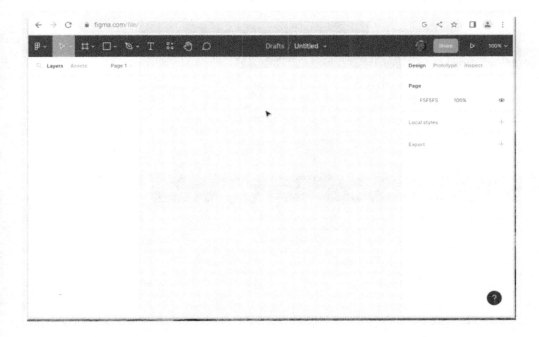

First, we're going to title our project. Click "Untitled", then give it a new name.

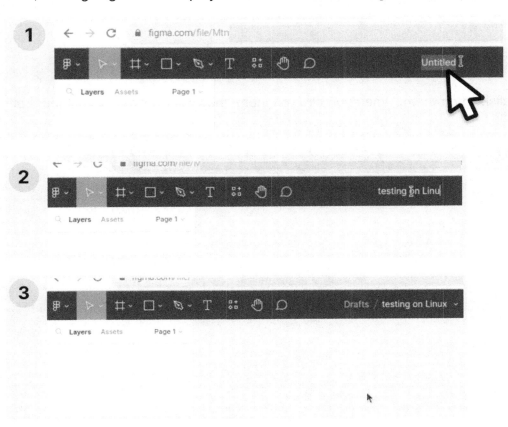

Intermission

Here are the top menu bar options.

The top bar

Let's create a square.

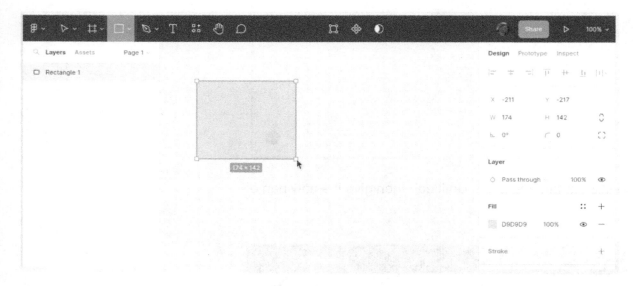

You can select different items by clicking on them. When you click on them, they will become highlighted; both on the canvas and in the left sidebar.

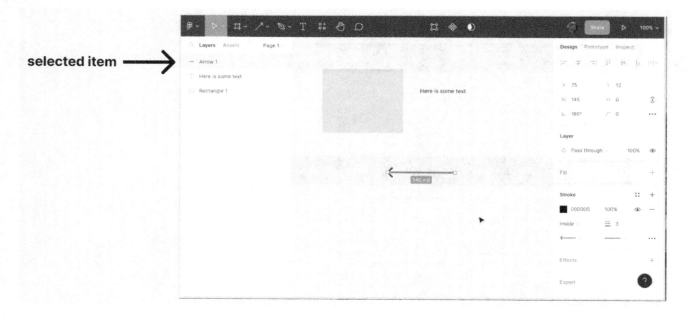

The right sidebar will show you the different options related to the object that you are working with.

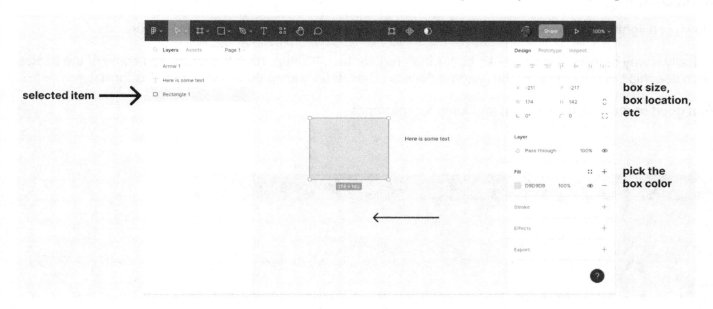

Here's a simplified breakdown of the workspace in Figma.

Sections Breakdown

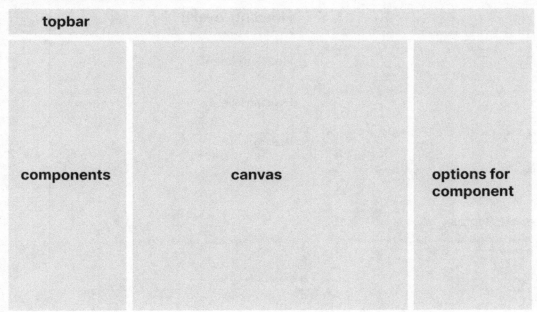

This little overview of Figma should help you get started with using it. Spend some time working with it and I promise you that it's going to be a tool that you will use often.

Markdown

Markdown is a lightweight markup language for creating formatted text using a plain-text editor.

It's basically a way to write text that looks better than regular text. It's important to understand some of the basics of how to use this because most of the readme docs on GitHub (including yours) will be in this format.

Here's a good starter link to checkout and keep for reference.

https://www.markdownguide.org/basic-syntax/

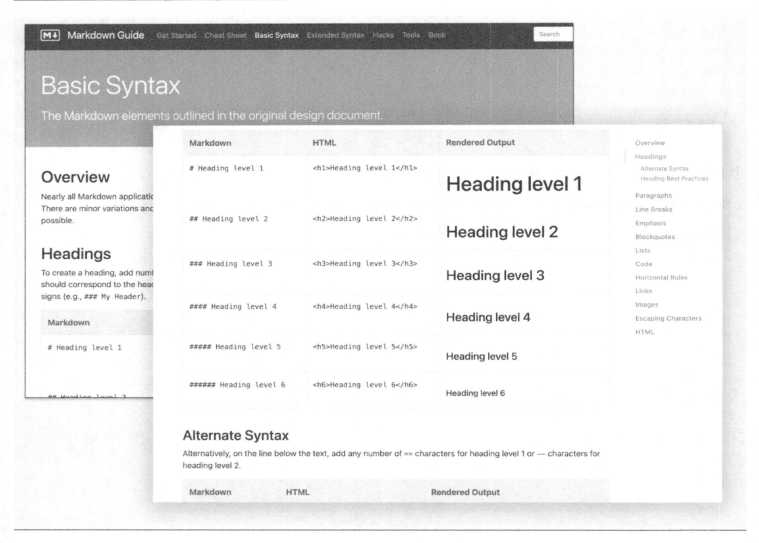

DOOM

Get the WAD File
Get the doom shareware WAD file.

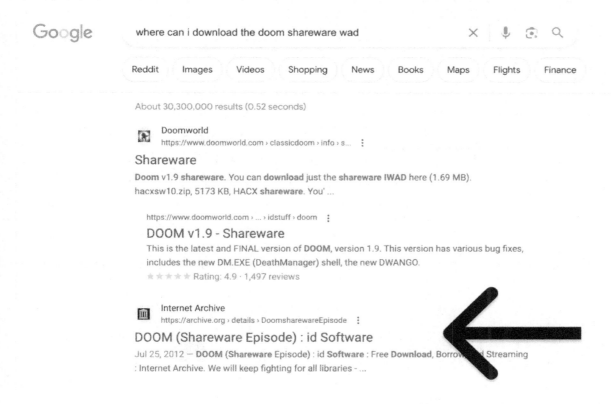

Look on the right side of the archive page under "download options". Then click ZIP.

Installing Crispy-Doom

We need to get Crispy-Doom installed now.

Open a new terminal window and change directory into downloads. Next, run the following commands.

```
$ cd Downloads
$ git clone https://github.com/fabiangreffrath/crispy-doom.git
```

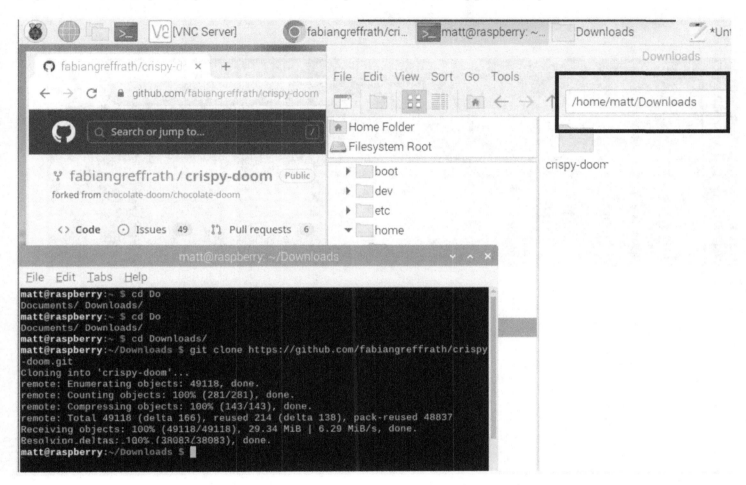

BTW, running "**git clone**" from the command line just downloads the repo to whatever directory you are currently in.

Intermission

If you've done it correctly, it will show up in the folder ("Downloads").

So far, we've downloaded the repo for crispy-doom, and we've downloaded the Doom wad file. Now we need to compile crispy doom to run on our system.

Go ahead and cd (change directory) into "crispy-doom".

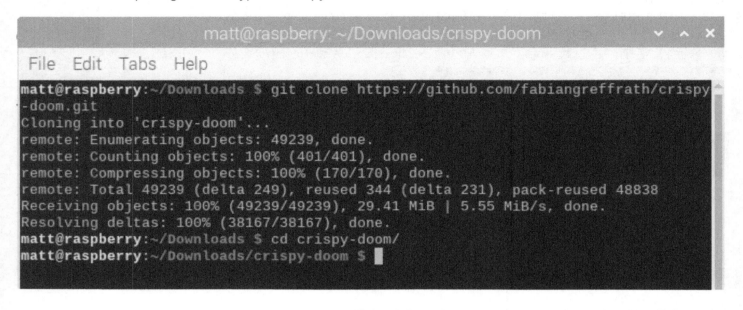

Compiling from source Explained

How do you play DOOM?

Well, DOOM originally came out for the PC, more specifically for MS-DOS in 1993.

Linux doesn't run DOS, so in order to play DOOM we need access to the source code. We can then compile that source code so that it can run on our system.

The doom engine is open source, this means that you can compile it yourself to make a binary.

What is compiling? It turns your code (human readable) into binary (0's and 1's), so that your computer can read the code.

What is a binary? In simple terms it's basically just like a .exe file in Windows.

Binaries are called binaries because they're just ones and zeros. Computers can run 1's and 0's very, very, fast.

In order to compile source code, we first need a few things...

Gcc
The next thing we need is the compiler this is called gcc. A compiler is a program that turns code into a binary. The package name for "gcc" is also gcc. This code will be compiled by "Make".

Make
Make is a tool used to compile multiple different code files into one larger binary package.

Auto configure
The next thing we'll need is auto configure, it creates a configure script that makes sure that you have all the necessary libraries or packages.

A library being some pre-made coding stuff that allows for rather complex things, things such as, creating a window to speed up and standardize development.

The package for auto configure is "auto conf".

Additional libraries
Finally, the last thing we need are the SDL libraries.

SDL stands for "simple direct media layer", it's a cross-platform software development library designed to provide a hardware abstraction layer for computer multimedia hardware components.

Bottom line is that we need these libraries on our machine in order to compile the code to get the game to run. Google "simple direct media layer" if you're interested in learning more about it.

Basically, it's an API that allows you to work with the computer without having to spend as much time writing code because a bunch of cool people already did that for us.

There are two types of SDL libraries.

"Regular" SDL libraries - are used by the actual programs themselves (think dependency - i.e., it needs it to run).

OR

"Dev" libraries - libraries used by developers, which are used by a compiler to build the code.

We will be installing both, there's multiple SDL libraries that Crispy Doom uses, so we need to install multiple packages.

The packages we need are:

Regular version < - - - - - > dev version
libsdl2-2.0-0 < - - - - - > libsdl2-dev
libsdl2-gfx-1.0-0 < - - - - - > libsdl2-gfx-dev
libsdl2-image-2.0-0 < - - - - - > libsdl2-image-dev
libsdl2-mixer-2.0-0 < - - - - - > libsdl2-mixer-dev
libsdl2-net-2.0-0 < - - - - - > libsdl2-net-dev

You can install all of these packages at once using this command:

```
$ sudo apt install libsdl2-2.0-0 libsdl2-dev libsdl2-gfx-1.0-0 libsdl2-gfx-dev
libsdl2-image-2.0-0 libsdl2-image-dev libsdl2-mixer-2.0-0 libsdl2-mixer-dev
libsdl2-net-2.0-0 libsdl2-net-dev
```

That's a ton of packages to install so I'd recommend going to this website to copy the text.

https://pastebin.com/JBgFMn2z

Compile Crispy-Doom

These are the commands that you need to run in order to get doom installed correctly. I'm going to list the commands for you to run step by step. Then I'm going to show you a screenshot of the expected output. Go ahead and run these commands along with me now.

Installing all the compiling stuff:
```
$ sudo apt install gcc make autoconf
```

Installing all the SDL2 Packages:
```
$ sudo apt install libsdl2-2.0-0 libsdl2-dev libsdl2-gfx-1.0-0 libsdl2-gfx-dev
libsdl2-image-2.0-0 libsdl2-image-dev libsdl2-mixer-2.0-0 libsdl2-mixer-dev
libsdl2-net-2.0-0 libsdl2-net-dev
```

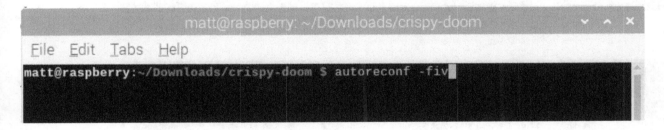

```
$ autoreconf -fiv
```

Setup

Intro

We're going to start with the easy way first by getting you set up with some remote desktop software. After we finish with that then we will be using SSH. You may need to read some documentation for this walkthrough, but I made it as easy as possible for you to get started. The reason for using remote desktop software first, is that I want you to understand how easy it is to connect to a different machine or server.

VNC

VNC stands for Virtual Network Computing. It's a screen sharing system that was created to remotely control another computer. This means that a computer's screen, keyboard, and mouse can be used from a distance by a remote user from a secondary device as though they were sitting right in front of it.

A VNC server is a program that shares a desktop with other computers over the Internet. For our purposes we will be using it on our local network so that we can connect to our workstation.

By using VNC you will be able to connect to your Linux machine remotely.

Depending on your workstation setup, you may need to download and install the programs to your machines directly. If you are using a Raspberry Pi, it should come pre-installed and ready to go because the Raspberry Pi Foundation has some deal with VNC. If you are running on a different system, then you will need to install the VNC Server on your workstation and VNC Viewer on your daily driver computer.

VNC Server
This runs on your remote machine (workstation). You need a VNC server if you want other people to see your desktop.

VNC Viewer
This runs on your local machine (daily driver). You need a VNC Viewer if you want to connect to a computer and view its desktop.

For Laptop
If you are running Linux (Raspbian) on an old computer or laptop, then you will need to go to the VNC Viewer website to download the software. After installing it, you can then just double click the icon in your downloads folder to then manually install the software. After the software finishes installing, go ahead and reboot your system.

> P.S. Whenever you make system wide changes to your machine it's often a good idea to reboot your machine. This is because sometimes but not always; system wide changes, in this case networking, will require a restart before those changes can take effect. I mention this because eventually, when you're working remotely, you may be scratching your head about why some setting is not taking effect. It's a good habit to train yourself to factor this in.

Intermission

This is what VNC Viewer looks like when running on your system.

This is a screenshot of the VNC Viewer app running on my mac. This is how I can remotely connect to my workstation from my mac.

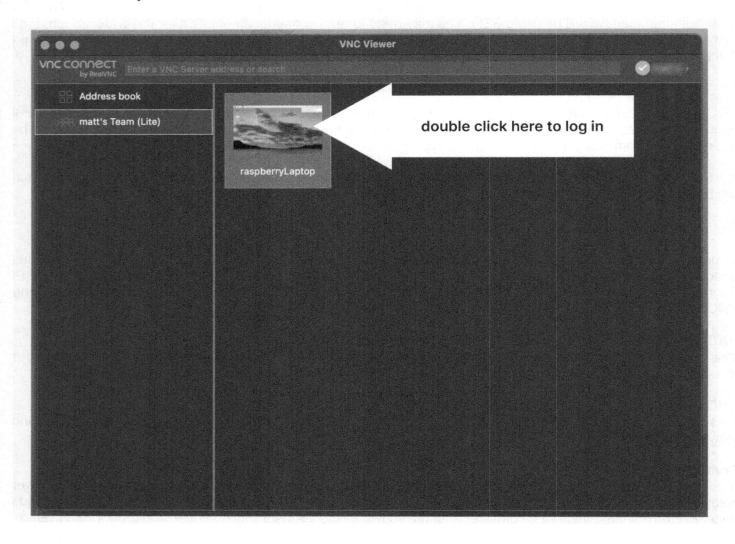

In order to log in you will need to enter your password. After you enter your password, a new screen will open to show you your desktop on your workstation that you are remotely connected to. How cool is that!

View from my mac

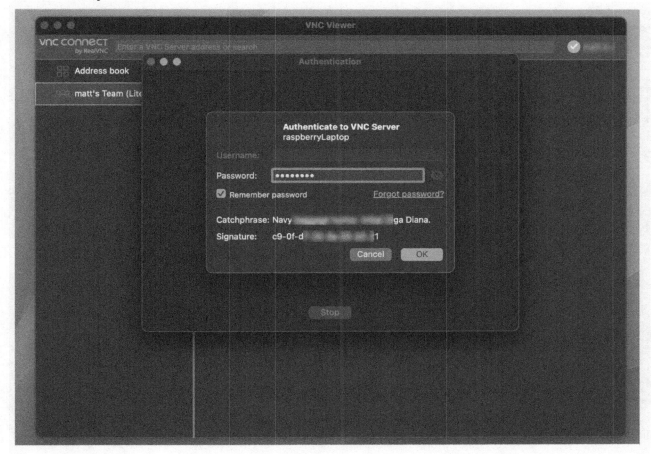

Intermission

This is what the VNC Server will look like when it's running on your workstation. After you have the VNC server running on your workstation. This is what connecting to my workstation laptop looks like when running VNC Viewer on my daily driver machine.

View from my mac

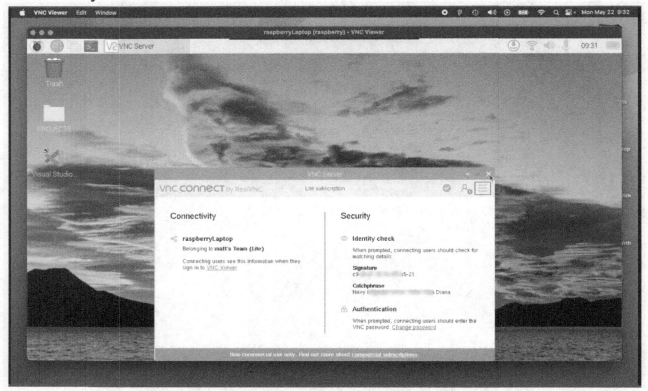

Additional options and settings

If you move your mouse cursor to the top of the window for the remote desktop, a menu with options will appear. You can do things like set the window to full screen, etc.

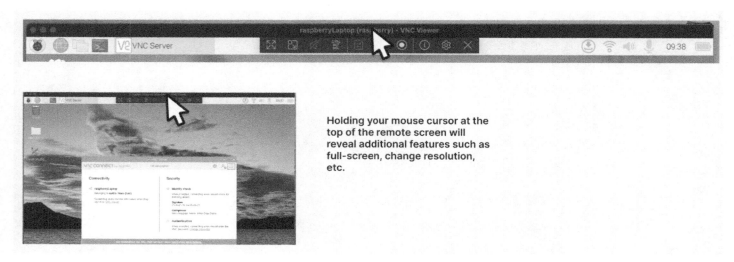

Holding your mouse cursor at the top of the remote screen will reveal additional features such as full-screen, change resolution, etc.

SSH

SSH or Secure Shell is a network communication protocol that enables two computers to communicate and share data. It allows you to connect to your Linux machine remotely. SSH has been used for almost 30 years to remotely work with Unix based systems.

Using SSH gives you access to the remote machine's command-line interface. Once you have access to a shell you can run commands as if you were sitting right at the machine.

Most servers are running Linux (Raspberry Pi, website hosts, etc.). With SSH you can do things like edit scripts, change .env files, configuration files and install software.

Bottom line - if you need to connect to a remote machine, SSH is what you'll be using.

Where there is a shell, there is a way.

How to enable SSH from the desktop (GUI Method)

Step 1

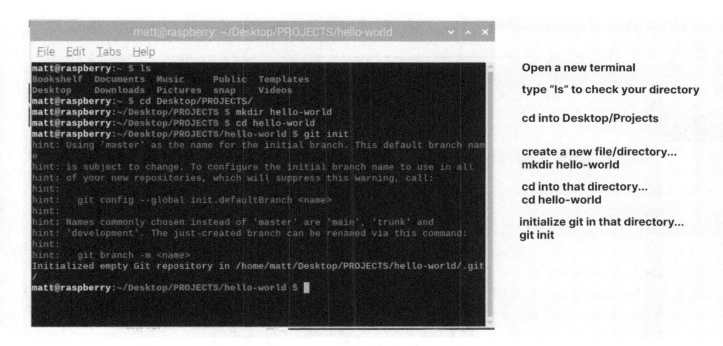

Open a new terminal

type "ls" to check your directory

cd into Desktop/Projects

create a new file/directory...
mkdir hello-world

cd into that directory...
cd hello-world

initialize git in that directory...
git init

Create 2 new files called index.html and hello.js. Then type "ls" to verify that they were created.

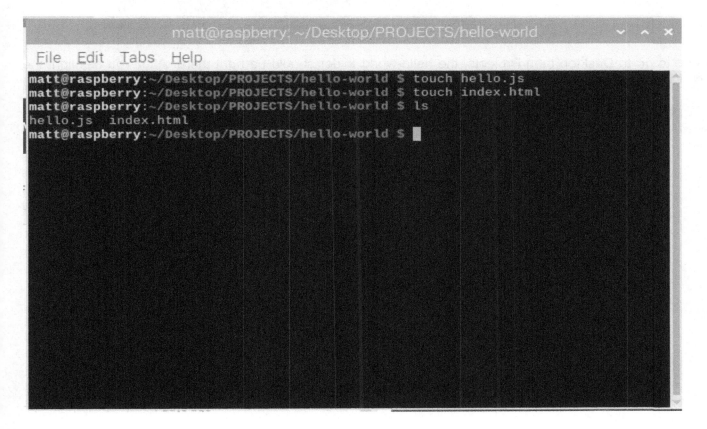

Intermission

Next open VS Code and open the folder.

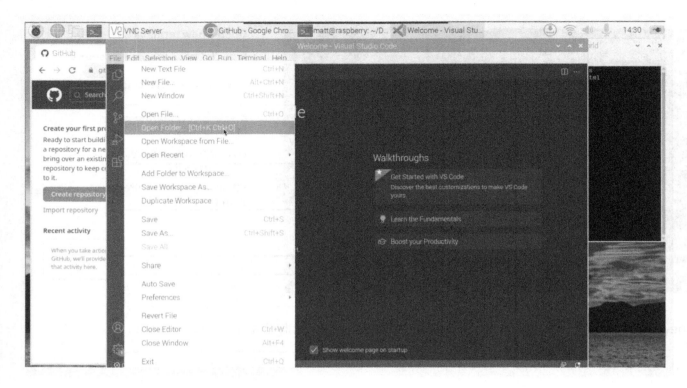

Remember to go to Desktop then Projects, the hello-world folder should be right there. After you highlight the folder, click the open button.

You should now see your project with the files inside of it.

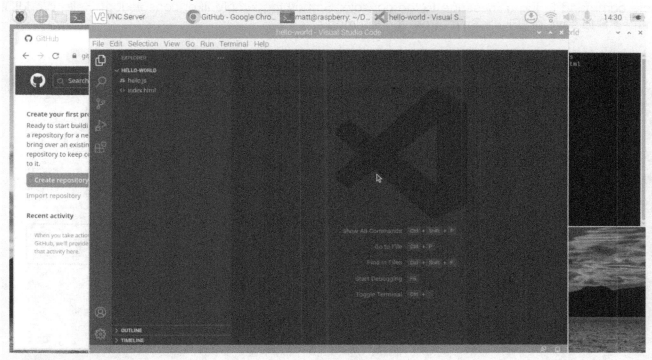

You may get a warning about trusting the files in this folder. You're the Author of this file so go ahead and click "Yes".

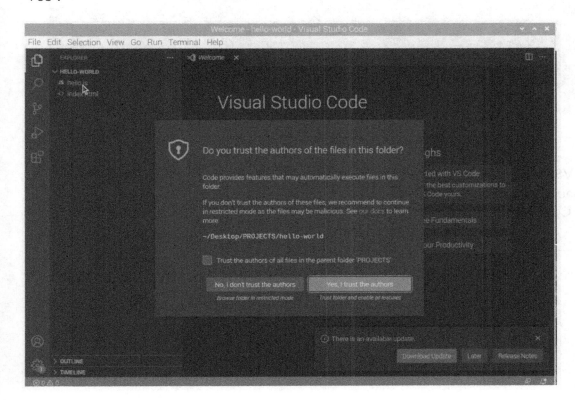

Intermission

Ok, now let's edit the file.

Add a console command to log a message to the console. Something simple like, console.log("Hello World!").

Then hit control + S to save or "File > Save" from the top menu.

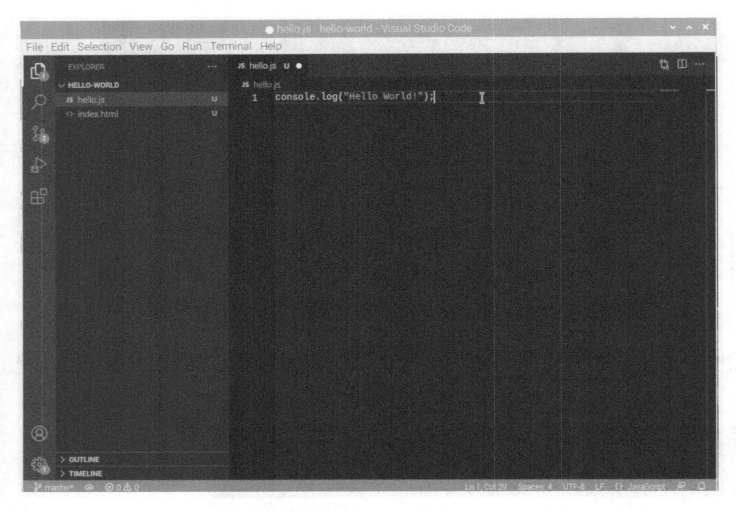

Sidenote

If you don't already have VS Code open and you want to view something in VS Code all you need to do is right-click and select "Visual Studio Code" and it will open the file in VS Code for you.

Paste your ssh public key into your GitHub account settings.

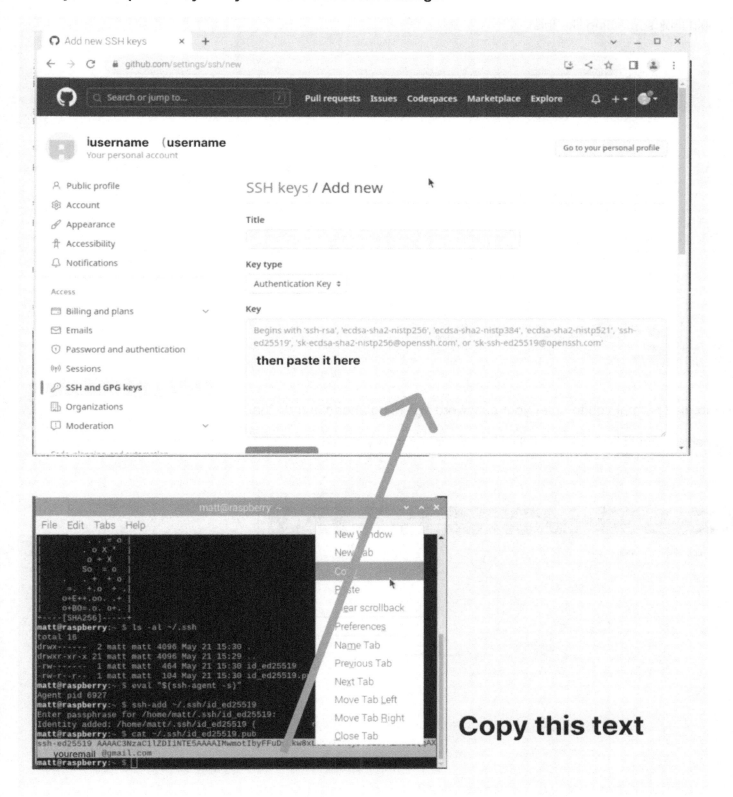

Intermission

Add a label (like "My laptop") and paste the public key into the big text box.

It should look something like this.

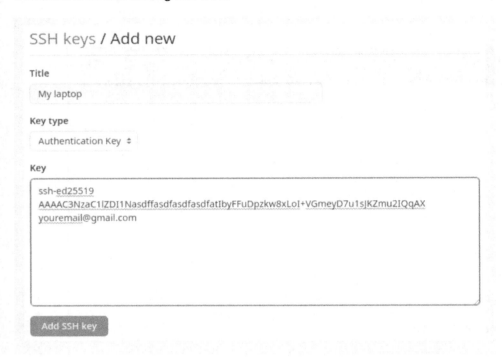

GitHub may prompt you to enter your password again, go ahead and do that.

This page should show up and will now have your ssh key added.

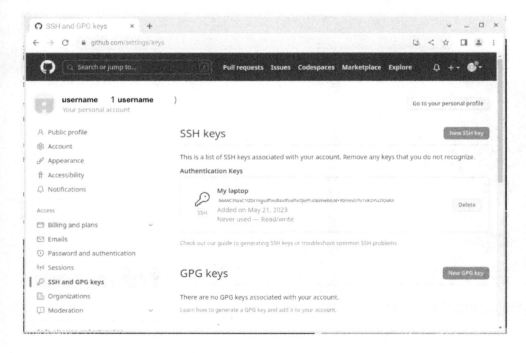

Testing to see if the keys worked

In a terminal/shell, type the following to test it:

```
$ ssh -T git@github.com
```

If it says something like the following, it worked:

Hi username! You've successfully authenticated, but GitHub does not provide shell access.

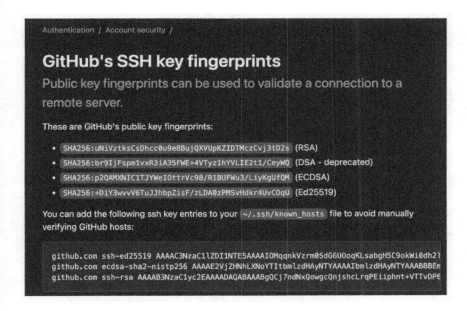

You can certify the fingerprint matches up by googling "githubs-ssh-key-fingerprints". You can look for the string of characters to see if they match.

Ok now that we have Git and GitHub setup let's make a new repo so that we can upload our code.

Making your first Repo

People usually refer to repositories as "repo's", pronounced as "re-poe".

In the top bar there is a plus sign with a carrot. Click that and then click on "New repository".

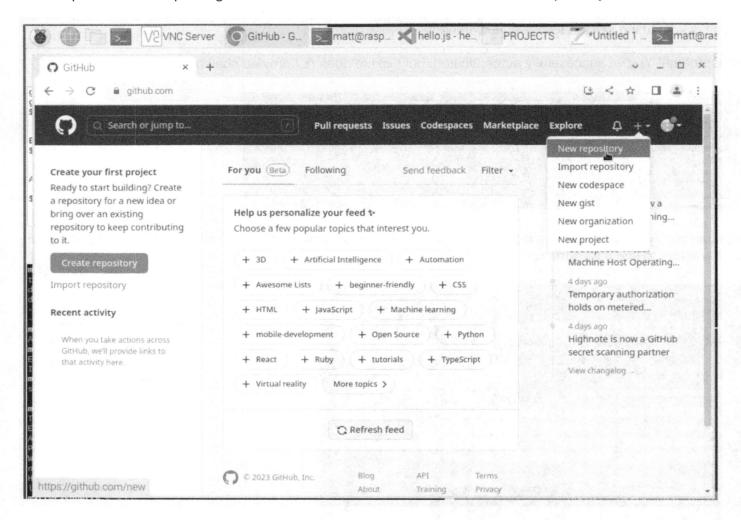

A new screen will appear.

Under the repository name, type in "hello-world", this is going to be the name of our repository.

You can set your repository to be **Public** or **Private**.

Just keep your stuff private for a while, you can always make it public later if you want to.

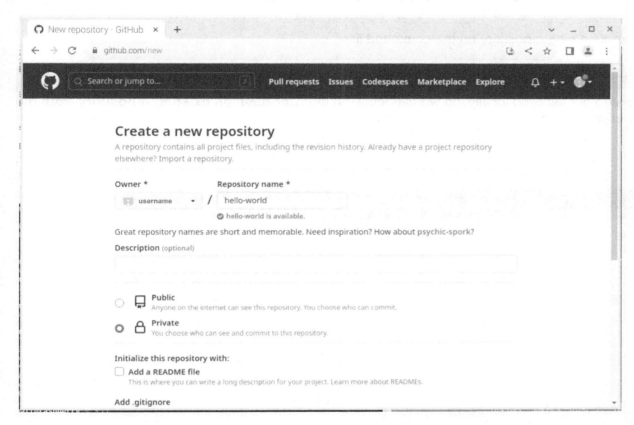

Scroll down to the bottom and click the button "Create repository".

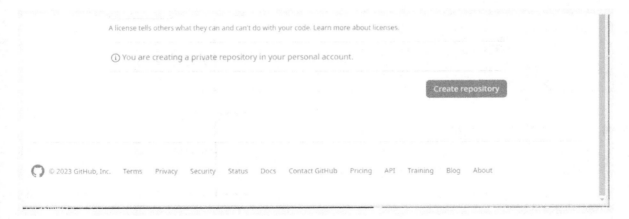

Intermission

After you click "Create repository", you're going to be brought to a new screen (it looks complicated so let's break it down).

Ok, so you have 2 options here:

Option 1

Ignore this "...or create a new repository on the command line"

Option 2

We've already created our Git repo locally, so we can focus on the **...or push an existing repository from the command line** section.

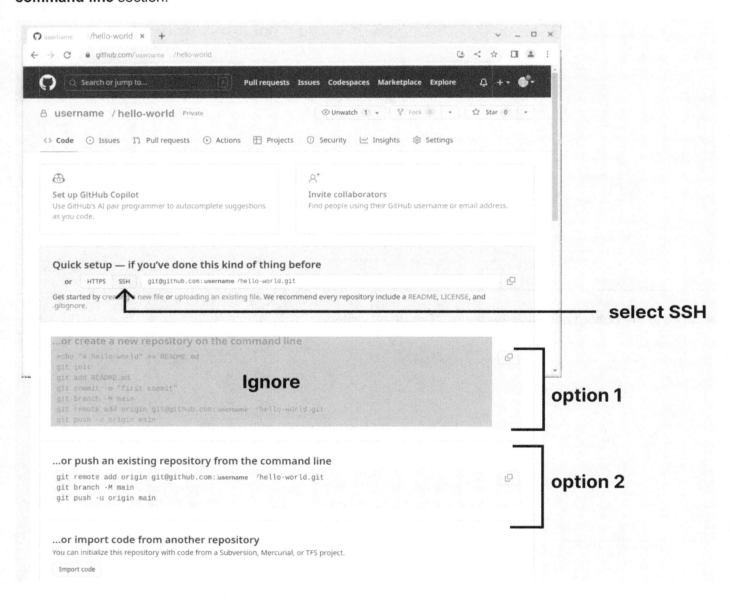

Click the copy button.

The 3 lines of code are now copied to your clipboard for you.

Paste those lines into your terminal under the directory where you are working (the place you initialized git).

```
matt@raspberry:~/Desktop/PROJECTS/hello-world $ git remote remove origin
matt@raspberry:~/Desktop/PROJECTS/hello-world $ git remote add origin git@github
.com:username./hello-world.git
matt@raspberry:~/Desktop/PROJECTS/hello-world $ git branch -M main
matt@raspberry:~/Desktop/PROJECTS/hello-world $ git push -u origin main
```

You will then be prompted to use the password for your keychain where the ssh key you made earlier is stored. If you password protected your keychain, then you will need to type that in (this password is most likely going to be different from your GitHub Account).

```
Enter passphrase for key '/home/matt/.ssh/id_ed25519':
Enumerating objects: 4, done.
Counting objects: 100% (4/4), done.
Delta compression using up to 4 threads
Compressing objects: 100% (2/2), done.
Writing objects: 100% (4/4), 284 bytes | 142.00 KiB/s, done.
Total 4 (delta 0), reused 0 (delta 0), pack-reused 0
To github.com:username /hello-world.git
 * [new branch]      main -> main
Branch 'main' set up to track remote branch 'main' from 'origin'.
matt@raspberry:~/Desktop/PROJECTS/hello-world $
```

Once that's done, you can go back to your browser, and you will see that your repo now has the updated files from your local repo. Pretty cool.

Step 2

Next, Scroll to the bottom of the next page. Under "Danger Zone" click "Change visibility" then "Change to public". You will Need to go through a confirmation prompt and enter your password.

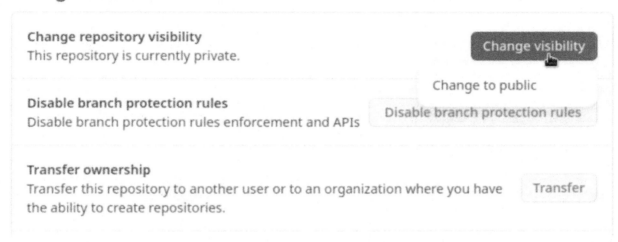

Step 3

In the sidebar click "Pages".

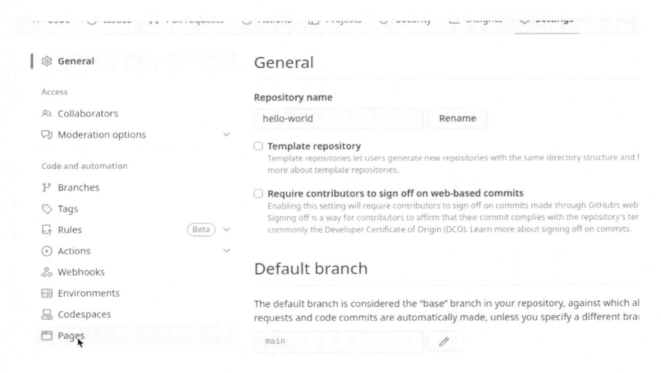

Intermission

Step 4

Next, click on "Branch", then pick "main".

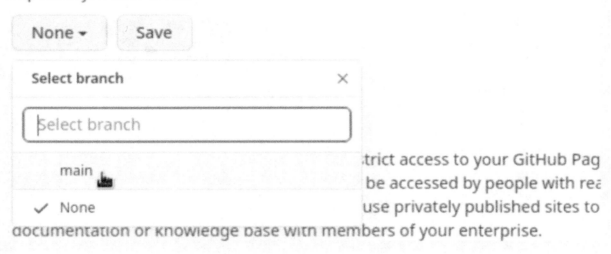

Step 5

Use the root folder, then click Save.

You should get a confirmation banner at the top of the page.

GitHub Pages source saved.

Step 6

You will need to wait a few minutes for the page to show up. Refresh your page and this should show up.

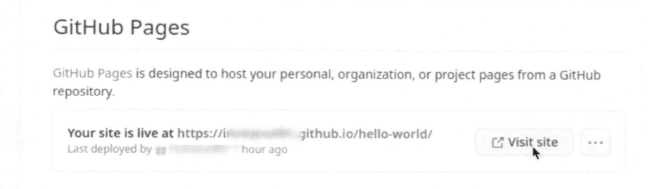

Step 7

To unpublish the site, just click the three-dot menu, then "unpublish site". Afterwards, you will see a banner at the top of the page confirming the site has been unpublished.

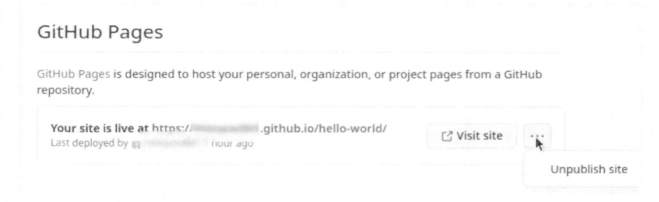

There is more that you can do with pages as well.

To learn more, you can go to https://docs.github.com/en/pages.

Project 1 - Weather App

Intro

We're going to build a little weather app together.

I'm going to walk you through the whole process from beginning to end.

My approach to teaching you in this way, is so that you can understand the following:
1. How web-based API's work
2. How to actually work with data from an API
3. Understand how to build something from a blank slate properly.

In order to use most web-based API's, you first have to sign up in order to get access to them. Most of these API's have a "free tier" version in order to get people to adopt them.

These "free tier" api's allow you to have a certain amount of api calls per day. To keep things simple, let's just assume that most offer 100 calls per day. If you exceed the limit of calls per day, it will cut you off.

This cut off usually shows up in the response from the api saying something like, "exceeded daily limit", "upgrade your subscription" or something similar like that. At that point, you can either wait until the next day or upgrade your account from free to paid.

About the API

I already went ahead and read through a bunch of the documentation and played around with the api.

Here's what I learned...

In order to get the current weather for an area, we first need a location. However, the weather api needs the latitude and longitude coordinates for the location in order to work.

Ok, cool, but the issue is that I don't know my latitude and longitude. I do, however, know what city I'm in.

So how do we get the latitude and longitude for the city?

Well, the Open Weather people accounted for this and made a "geocoding" api.

In a nutshell, "geocoding" is the process of converting a location, address or place, into geographic coordinates. These coordinates typically consist of latitude and longitude values, which can pinpoint a location on the Earth's surface.

Essentially, the geocoding api takes a city and gets the latitude and longitude for it. After the api finds the location, it then returns a response back to us with the info we need (requested).

How the program is going to work

1. Call geocoding api
2. Get latitude and longitude
3. Save latitude and longitude somewhere
4. Call weather api
5. Get weather data
6. Show current temperature

Easy enough... Let's go.

If you want, you can create a little to do list in a separate notepad and track your progress. This is how I usually work.

```
File   Edit   Search   View   Document   Help

                        Untitled 1

How the program is going to work
[] Call geocoding api
[] Get latitude and longitude
[] Save latitude and longitude somewhere
[] Call weather api
[] Get weather data
[] Show current temperature
```

Having a check list works great because it allows you to keep focused on what you're doing or need to do. You don't have to stop and think, you can just work through your check list and make progress.

Spend 5-10 minutes making a to-do list and you will save yourself hours in the long run.

Geocoding API endpoint

Ok, now that you've checked out the documentation lets scroll down a bit and see if we can find the "geocoding api".

It's located about halfway down the page here: https://openweathermap.org/api. Try to find it on your own. That said, I took a screenshot and dropped a big arrow for you so that you can't miss it.

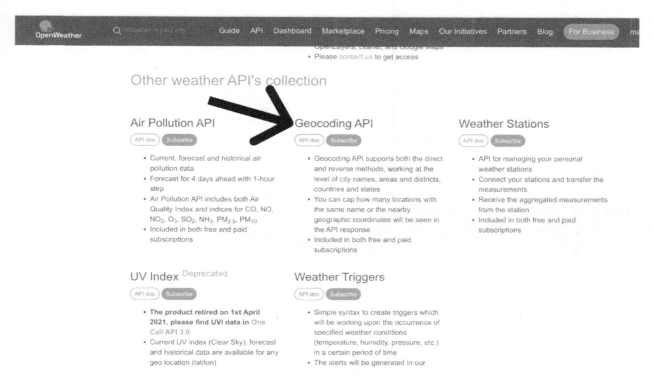

When you find the geocoding api, go ahead and click on that.

It's a little confusing, so just click the button titled "API doc", you can ignore the "Subscribe" button.

Project 1 - Weather App

It should take you to this page: https://openweathermap.org/api/geocoding-api. Take a minute to read the description. When you're done, move on to the next step.

Scroll down on that page until you see something like this.

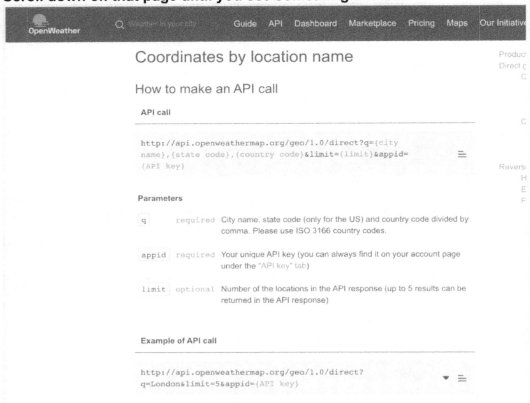

This documentation is really good. It tells you how to make an api call, it shows you what parameters it takes, and it also gives you an example. Very nice :)

Endpoint, parameters and values

If you look at the section titled "Example of API call", you will see a string inside of a little box, see photo.

Example of API call

```
http://api.openweathermap.org/geo/1.0/direct?
q=London&limit=5&appid={API key}
```

This might be your first time looking at something like this, so I made a little breakdown for you in order to help you understand what you're looking at.

When you are reading the string (URL), this is how you should view it in your mind. It has 3 parameters with 3 values.

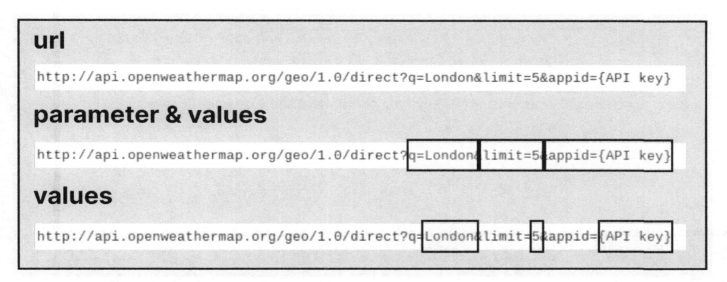

If you look at the documentation, under the "How to make an API call" > "Parameters" section, you should see that the parameters in the documentation match up with the URL.

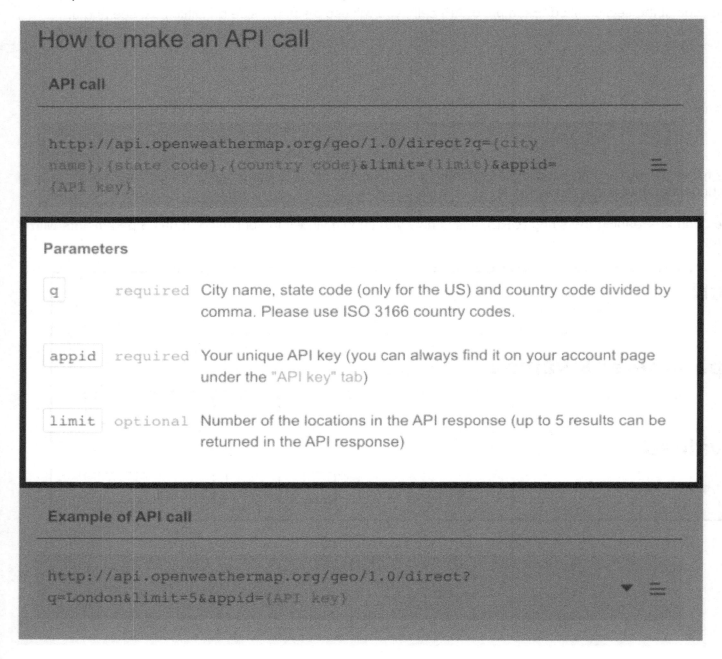

You should now see the results from the query again but this time the response is formatted much better.

After using the JSON viewer extension

Notice how much cleaner and easier it is to read that?

That's why this extension is awesome.

Get Coordinates

One last thing before we move on, the whole point of using this "geocoding" api was so that we could get our coordinates. Let's copy ours now so that we can use them later.

Highlight the text like I did, then "right-click", copy. You're looking for the "lat" and "lon" strings with the numbers next to them.

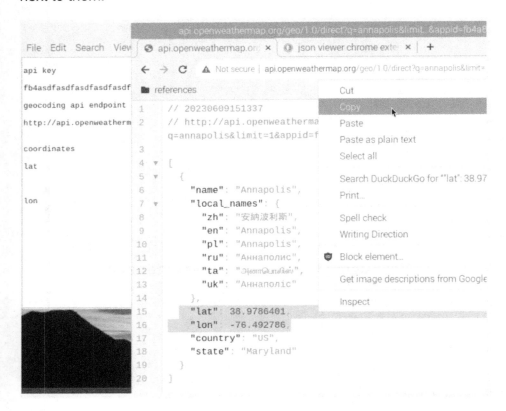

Go to your notepad and paste your coordinates there.

Here's how your notes should look (I cleaned mine up a little).

After you have your coordinates in your notes you can move on to the next step.

What is JSON?

JSON is one of the ways that you can send data back and forth over the internet. It's also one of the ways databases can return results to you as well (more on that later).

For now, just understand that when we're using an api, we expect the data that we get returned to us to be formatted in a way that we can easily parse the data.

Parse is just a fancy term for "how a computer reads some data".

JSON is a widely used and adopted way of formatting and moving data around. Most languages that you use (Python, JavaScript, etc.), have built in ways of working with that data. We're going to get into how to "parse" and work with this data pretty soon. So, stay with me, because this is all going to make a lot more sense soon.

Here's the official website if you want to learn more about JSON: https://www.json.org/.

Weather API endpoint

We still need to be able to check the weather, so let's get this weather query setup.

In your browser go back to the main api documentation page here: https://openweathermap.org/api.

You can either type in that URL or just click in the navbar here:

Here's the main API page that you should be on now.

When you get there, scroll down just a little bit until you reach the section that says, "Current Weather Data".

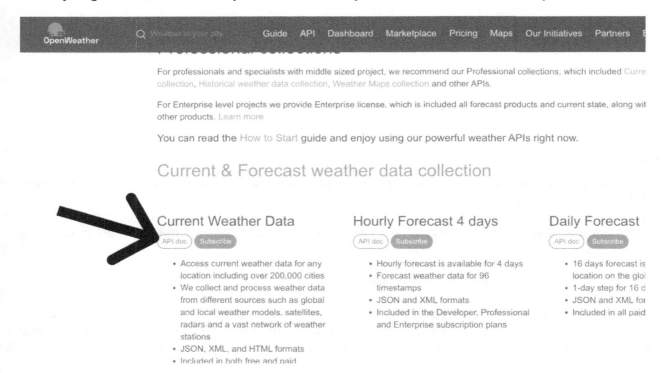

Go ahead and click on the "API doc" button that the arrow is pointing to.

Now you should be at the documentation page for the "Current Weather Data" api. The URL should be https://openweathermap.org/current.

See if you can find the URL for the endpoint that we are going to be querying.

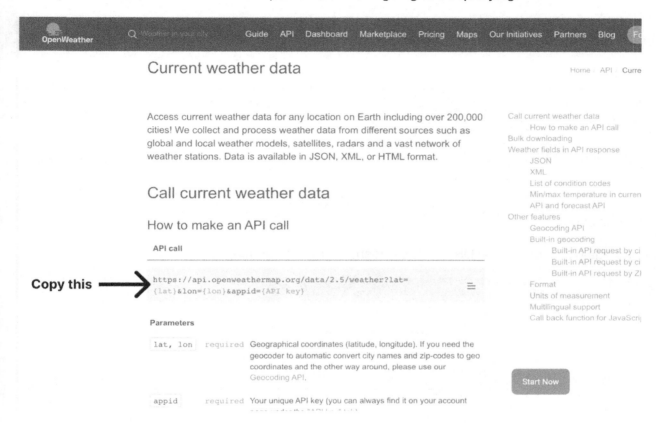

We're looking for something like "how to make an api call". While you're here, take a few minutes to skim through the documentation. Sometimes there's other cool features that you might not have known existed.

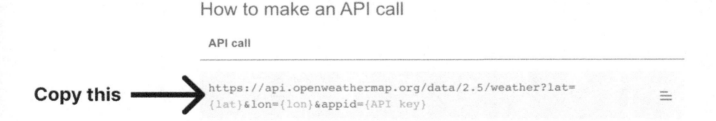

Here's the URL with the parameters we need to fill out. Notice how this documentation is so awesome that they color coded the different parameters for us? Pretty sweet.

Project 1 - Weather App

Here's a list of the parameters that we can work with.

Parameters

`lat, lon`	required	Geographical coordinates (latitude, longitude). If you need the geocoder to automatic convert city names and zip-codes to geo coordinates and the other way around, please use our Geocoding API.
`appid`	required	Your unique API key (you can always find it on your account page under the "API key" tab)
`mode`	optional	Response format. Possible values are `xml` and `html`. If you don't use the `mode` parameter format is JSON by default. Learn more
`units`	optional	Units of measurement. `standard`, `metric` and `imperial` units are available. If you do not use the `units` parameter, `standard` units will be applied by default. Learn more
`lang`	optional	You can use this parameter to get the output in your language. Learn more

Let's get this query finished...

Open your notepad again and paste that URL in there. It should look something like this now.

```
*Untitled 1 - Mousepad

File  Edit  Search  View  Document  Help

api key

fb4a8cfaa9164df205a3c8c0c0f0c8b6

geocoding api endpoint

http://api.openweathermap.org/geo/1.0/direct?q=annapolis&limit=5&appid=fb4a8cfaa9164df205a3c8

coordinates

"lat": 38.9786401
"lon": -76.492786

weather api endpoint

https://api.openweathermap.org/data/2.5/weather?lat={lat}&lon={lon}&appid={API key}
```

You should see your new project folder on your desktop now.

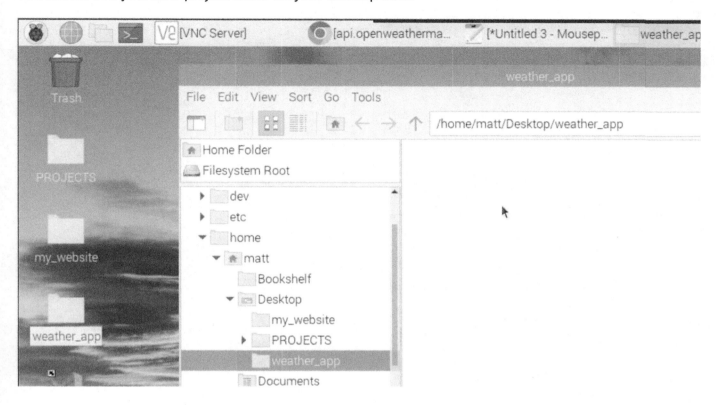

Now make the following files
- index.html
- style.css
- script.js

Project 1 - Weather App

You can either right-click inside the folder and create a new file for each of those files or you can follow the next method.

Method 1

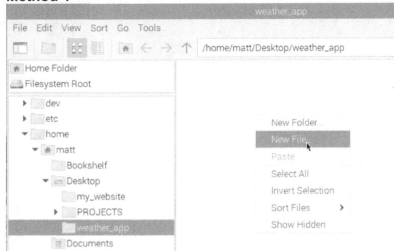

Method 2

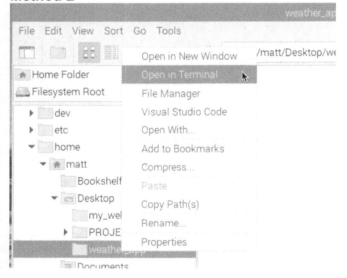

Use the touch command, using this command will create a file for you. You can create multiple files at the same time. The touch command creates files in whatever directory you are currently in.

Using the touch command
```
$ touch somefile.txt someotherfile.html
```

```
matt@raspberry:~/Desktop/weather_app $ touch index.html style.css script.js
```

Here's how your folder should look with the 3 files in it.

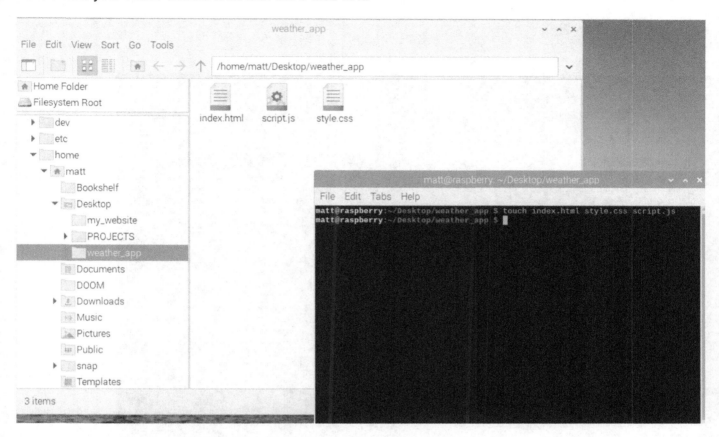

Now open your project in vscode, right-click on the folder and select "Visual Studio Code".

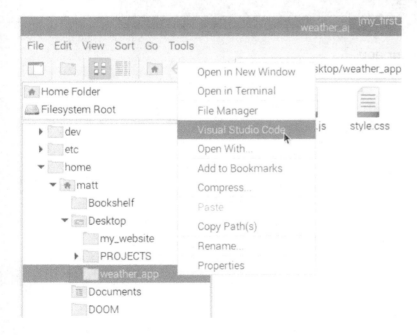

Project 1 - Weather App

Here's what your project should look like in vscode.

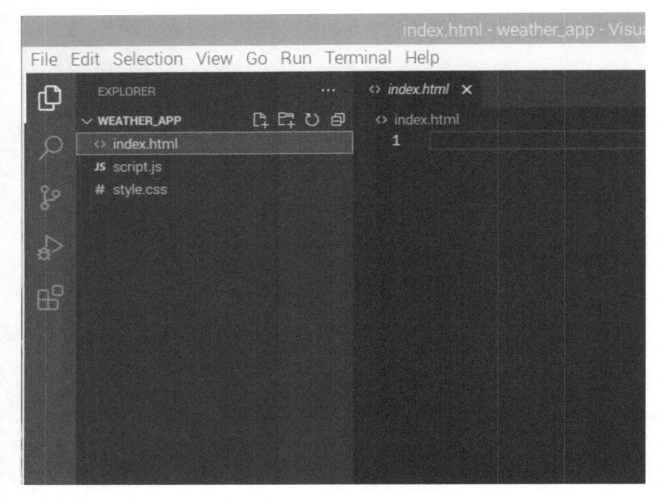

Alright, now we're ready to get started with building our app.

HTML

Open your web browser and go to w3schools (). Then click on the HTML tab.

Copy the html example code, you can find the code snippet/example in the sidebar under the "HTML HOME" tab.

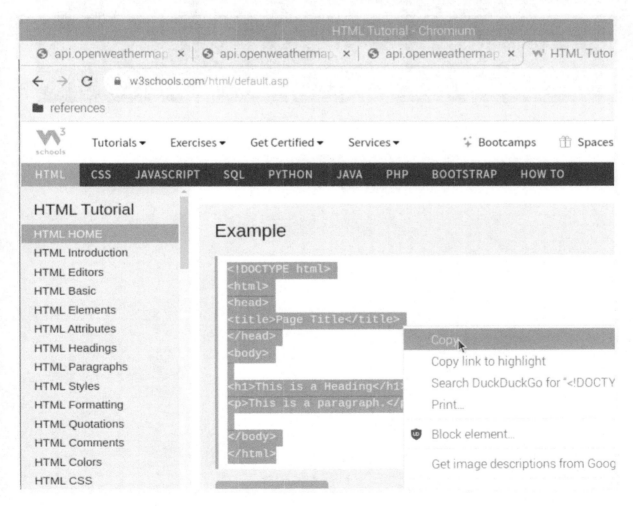

Project 1 - Weather App

Paste the example code in your editor, then change the title and the text. Here's what mine looks like.

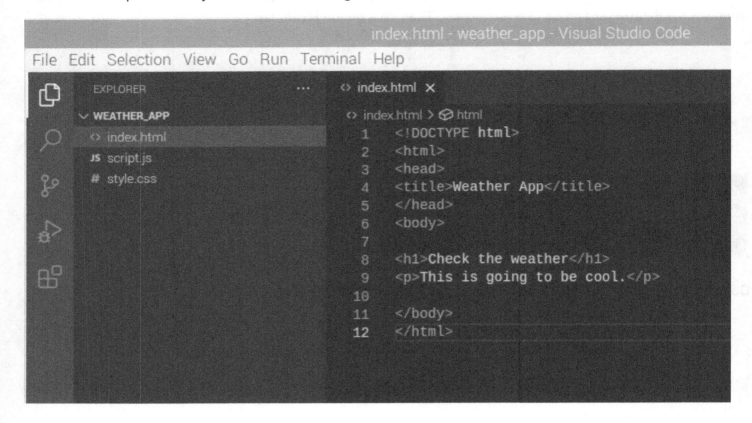

CSS

Remember earlier how we included our CSS and JavaScript files into our web page? Well, we need to do that again. Go ahead and do that now.

If you need a hint for how to do it, you can go to w3schools, then click the "HTML CSS" tab in the side menu. Scroll down to External CSS and you can grab a code snippet from the example.

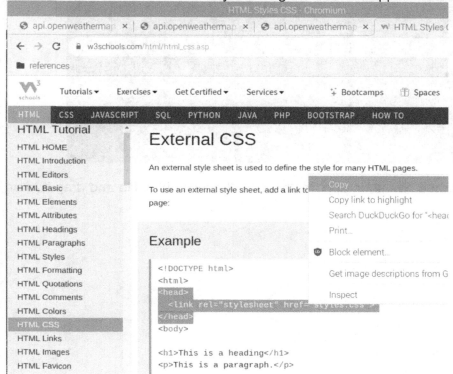

Here's how my index.html page looks now.

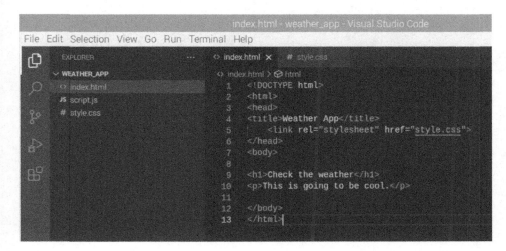

Picking up the pace

Ok, I'm going to pick up the pace a little bit more now. I'll still continue to guide you and at the end of this chapter I'll also include all of the code so that you can reference it.

That said, I'm counting on you to count on yourself. You can do this.

Readme file

In your sidebar right click and create a readme file. Personally, I use these as a way to include notes or whatever other relevant info related to the thing I'm building that I need.

I'm putting my "to-do list" and my URLs from my notepad notes in there. This way things will be more organized when I come back to the project 6 months later and I've totally forgotten about everything. By standardizing the readme documentation like this - i.e., being part of every project that I build, I will always have a good reference or jumping off point when I come back to a project. Also, if I decide to share the project with someone later, they also will have a place to start off from.

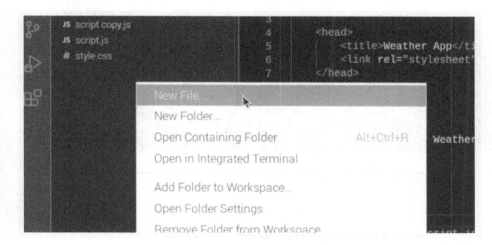

Make sure to type: readme.md, the ".md" extension stands for markdown. It's a better file format than just plaintext.

Project 1 - Weather App

Copy your notes from the text editor

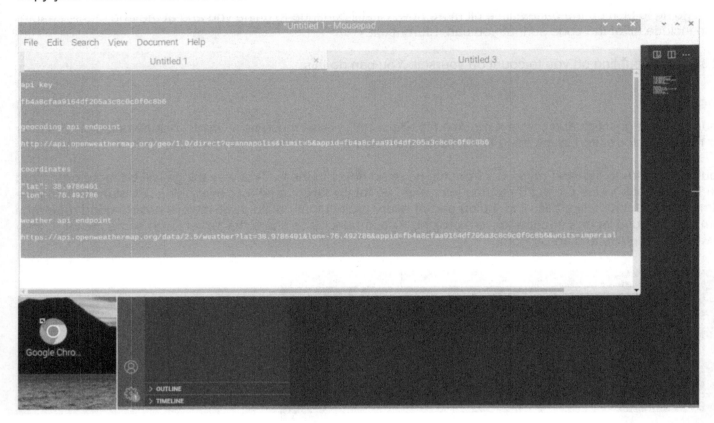

Paste your notes in to the readme file

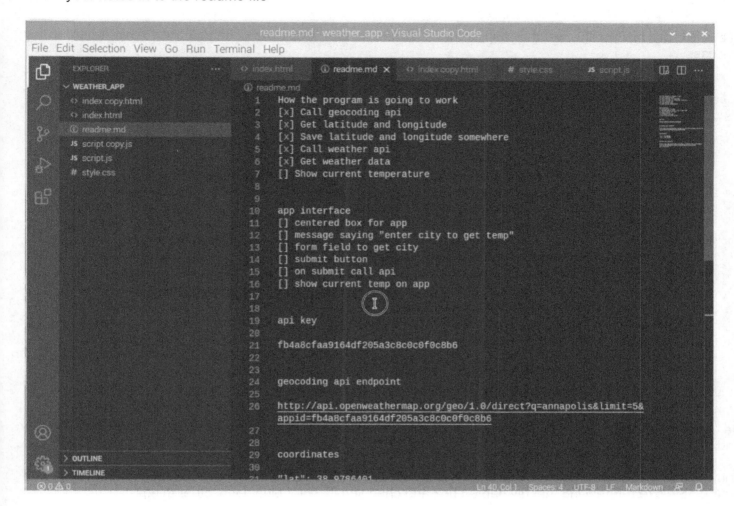

Continuing on

Let's make our box for the weather app show up on the screen. Copy the code just like I have it here in my style.css.

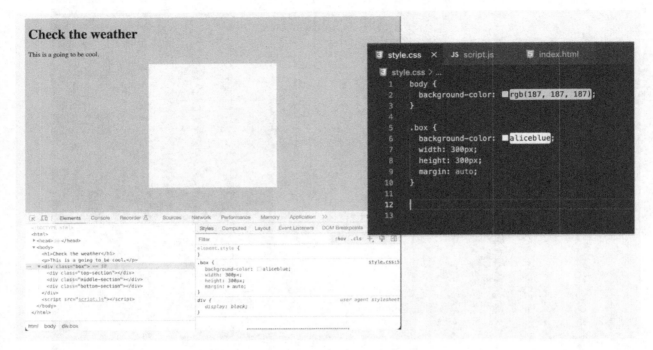

The ".box" means that we are targeting the "box class". Remember how we gave the div for our box a name? We used the "class" attribute.

I know, it's a lot to take in right now, just try to draw the correlation that in our html we named the div "box", and in our CSS we're referencing that div named box and changing its color plus a few other things.

Trust me, if you work with this a little bit you'll understand.

I also gave the box a width and a height.

You can see the structure of how this works is:

thing: setting;

The main thing to understand here is:
1. There's a basic structure or format to how you write CSS.
2. There are so many rules that you have to look them up based on what you are trying to do.

For you to get a good understanding of how to work with CSS I would recommend you use this reference on w3schools; it's straightforward and searchable.

Click the CSS Tab in the navbar, scroll down the sidebar and find the "CSS References" section.

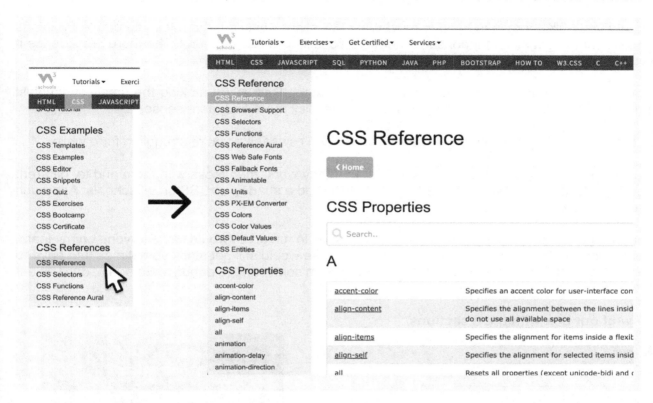

For example, if I wanted to learn how to use the "min-width" property, I would just look it up and then mess around with the code example for a little bit. Once I got a grasp of how to use it, I would bring it into my codebase. Rinse and repeat and you're now styling your HTML page.

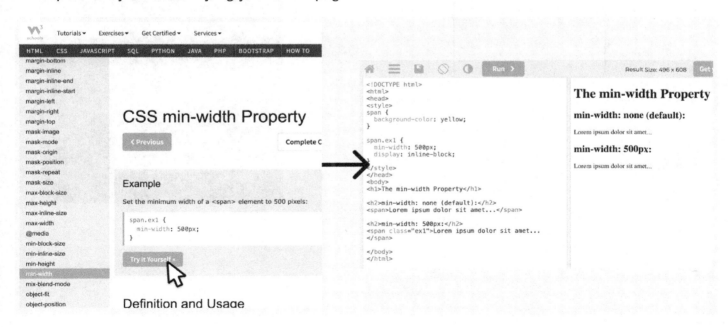

Project 1 - Weather App

CSS is a lot to take in, there's so many rules and settings. Plus, there's also a lot of gotchas.

The basic gist to get you 50% there is to keep in mind that CSS styles cascade, the rules you create for things flow down like a river (not to get all metaphorical). The more specific you get with a rule the more precedence it has over other rules. You can also combine rules, which I'll show you later.

Don't get too caught up in CSS if you get stuck (you will get stuck). Rather, try making the smallest simplest changes to things, then, over time as you use it, CSS will start to click more and more sense.

Of all the things to learn, this one can just break your brain. So don't sweat it if you're struggling for a while.

My final bit on this is to just copy my code examples. Test that they work, *then* mess with them and try different things out. Try adding a shadow to the box by looking up how to add a shadow in CSS on w3schools. Approach learning CSS like that.

For context, I once worked for a company where we fixed websites to run ads. I would say everyone on my team, like 10 of us, were in the top 10% of CSS developers out there. We would still get stuck sometimes and have to throw a code screenshot in a Slack chat to get a bunch of people on something to debug it. So again, don't sweat this too hard.

Side by side view of our box with the 3 sections

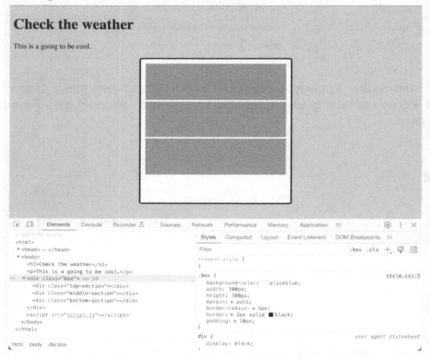

Browser view of our box with the 3 sections (note: dev tools shows the styles for the box)

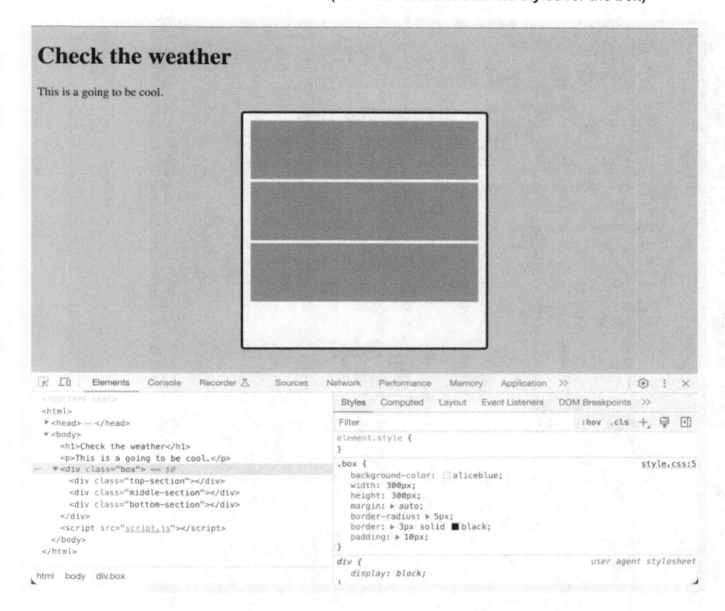

Back to our code, let's open up the script.js file. Go ahead and paste in, this code:

```
document.getElementById("city").value;
```

Just because we added this code to our script.js file doesn't mean it will do anything yet.

Let's now go to our browser and type a city into our input. Then, after you enter a city, open dev tools (Shift + CTRL + J or right-click > inspect). In dev tools, click console and then paste that same code in there and hit Enter.

You should see something like this.

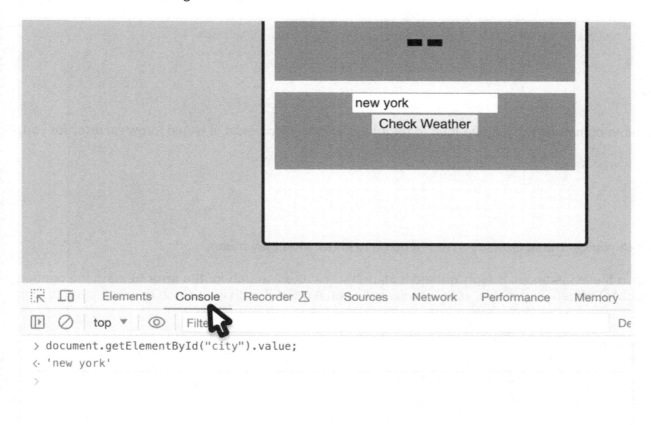

Ok, sweet. Now that we know that the code snippet works, let's make the "Check Weather" button work so that when we click it, it will get the text value for us from the input.

Project 1 - Weather App

Using the console

Notice how after you hit enter, the city appears in red text in the console?

This is because the console in dev tools runs as a JavaScript interpreter. The cool thing about the console is that it allows you to interact with the web page through the console.

You can run any JavaScript command that you want here, it's great for testing out ideas quickly or finding out how to target different elements.

Here's the code that we just ran. As you can see, it checked the document (our HTML file), then it found the element with the "id" of "city", then it got the value (the text we entered) and it returned that value to the console.

```
> document.getElementById("city").value;
<- 'new york'

>
```

If you took that same command but instead tried to target an "id" that didn't exist, it would throw an error for you.

```
> document.getElementById("doesnt-exist").value;
❌ ▶ Uncaught TypeError: Cannot read properties of null (reading 'value')
       at <anonymous>:1:40
> |
```

A lot of times when you get these errors, you're not going to know what they mean.

What you can do in these instances is highlight the text, right-click, then search for the error through the context menu (see screencap). When you do this, your browser will open a new tab with the search results for you to look at.

Look up error in Google.

Research error

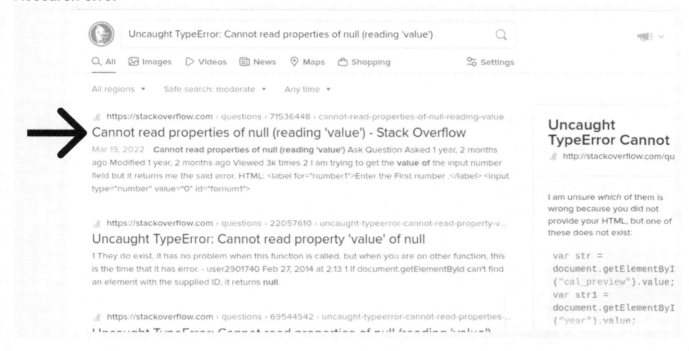

Clearing the console

If you have a bunch of errors in your console it can fill up fast, to clear your console, just hit this button.

Cleared console

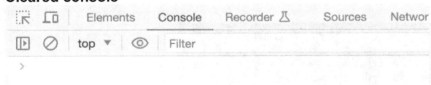

Project 1 - Weather App

Making the button work

When we click the button we want our program to grab the city and dump it to the console.

Here's how it should work:
1. Click button
2. Call function
3. Function grabs text input
4. Function returns value to console

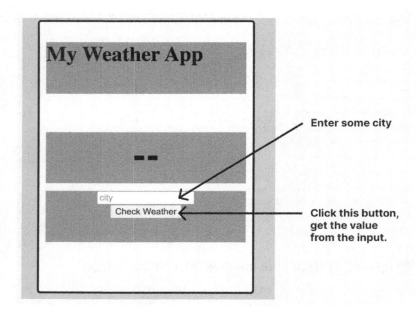

Open up your HTML file and go to the input, replace this code in there.

old

```
<button class="btn" onclick="alert('button clicked')">
    Check Weather
</button>
```

new

```
<button class="btn" onclick="getWeather()">
    Check Weather
</button>
```

Go ahead and try the button out again after you've replaced the code.

If your console is open, you will see you get a new error.

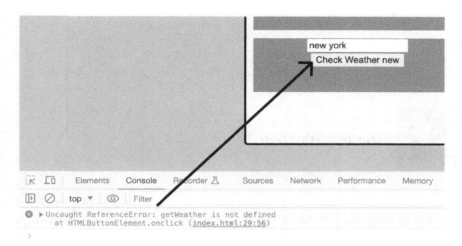

Getting the name of the city won't work yet because we told the button to call a function that doesn't exist yet - i.e., the button works but the function is missing.

We need to make that new function now.

I pulled two snippets from the html file and the script file for you to look at. I want you to make the association of how these two things are connected.

function call from onClick event for button in the HTML file

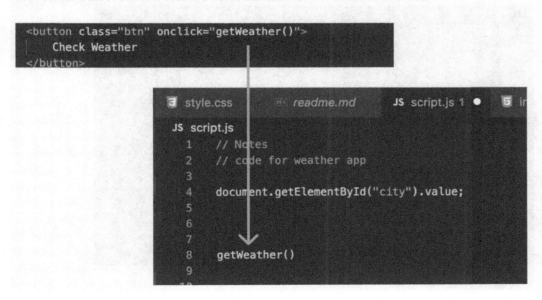

You should notice some similarities here... This isn't exactly correct, it's more like pseudocode. Just recognize that we are calling the function by its name followed by some parentheses like this, "getWeather()". The name of the function is the same in both the HTML and the JavaScript file.

Step 4
Rearrange and clean up our code, your code should look like this now.

```js
// Notes
// code for weather app

function getWeather() {
  var city = document.getElementById("city").value;

  var location = getLocation(city);

  console.log(location);
}

function getLocation(city) {
  var location_data = `lat/lon data for: ${city}`;

  return location_data;
}
```

Output after you enter city and click button

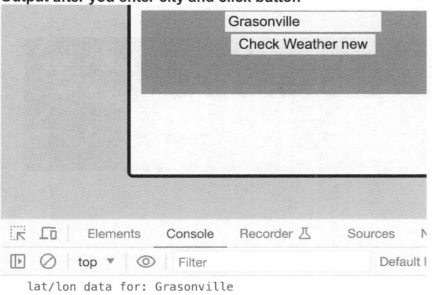

```
lat/lon data for: Grasonville
>
```

Project 1 - Weather App

Our getWeather() function has two variables, city and location.

When we call the function it grabs the city from the input.

It then moves down and gets the location with the value from the city variable.

The location variable is set to the output from the return statement of the getLocation() function.

If this is confusing, it's ok, it's hard to talk about programming in a text explanation, it's just one of those things where you have to do it to understand it.

"There's a difference between knowing the path and walking the path".

- Morpheus

Step 5
Getting some data.

We're going to add our URL inside of our getLocation() function.

Notice that we are using string interpolation inside of our URL string.

This is so we can pass the city variable inside of that string.

Next, we're using a new function called fetch(), it takes the URL as a parameter.

We're changing the output of our "location_data" now by telling it to parse the JSON data that we get back from the fetch() function.

```
function getLocation(city) {
  var url = `http://api.openweathermap.org/geo/1.0/direct?q=${city}&limit=1&appid=fb4a8cfaa9164df205a3c8c0c0f0c8b6`;

  const location = fetch(url);

  const location_data = location.json();

  return location_data;
}
```

Now when we test our program out again, we should see some new output.

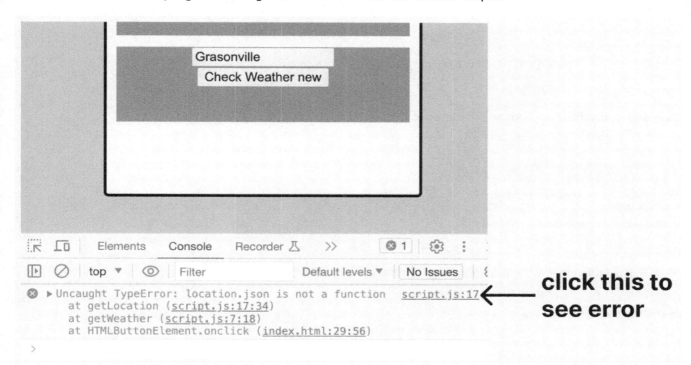

Viewing the error in the console

```
11
12  function getLocation(city) {
13    var url = `http://api.openweathermap.org/geo/1.0/direct?q=${ci
14
15    const location = fetch(url);
16
17    const location_data = location.json();  ⊗
18
19    return location_data;
20  }
21
22  // async function getLocation(city) {
```

❌ Uncaught TypeError: location.json is not a function

▼ Threads
➧ Main

▼ Breakpoints
☐ Pause on uncaught ex
☐ Pause on caught exce

▼ Scope

This error is a little confusing and difficult to figure out and track down. However, I copied the location.json() that was highlighted by the red squiggles and asked google about it. It gave me this Mozilla link that had a great little review and explanation for me to learn about how or why I might have gotten this error. A lot of times in programming the answers aren't immediately obvious, sometimes you just need to spend an hour or more learning some new concept - it's just part of programming. We never stop learning; we just keep getting better.

Project 1 - Weather App

Looking up the error and understanding .json()

Reading through this doc, explained promises a little bit. So, I'm going to go to w3schools now and see what I can find.

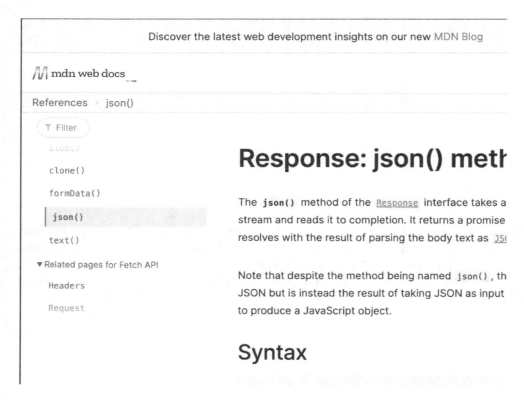

Finished Code

There's 3 function we need to make this program work (I collapsed the code so it would fit in the screenshot)

```js
JS script.js > ...
  1    // Notes
  2    // code for weather app
  3
  4  > async function getWeather() {...
 51    }
 52
 53  > async function getLocation(city) {...
 61    }
 62
 63  > async function getWeatherData(location_data) {...
 74    }
 75    |
```

The next few pages show the expanded views.

Project 1 - Weather App

Function for getWeather

```
4    async function getWeather() {
5        // get the value from the input
6        var city = document.getElementById("city").value;
7
8        // get the location data for the city from the api
9        const location_data = await getLocation(city);
10
11       // get the current weather data for the city from the api
12       const weather_data = await getWeatherData(location_data);
13
14       // update the display
15
16       // set temp
17       document.getElementById("degrees").innerHTML =
18         Math.floor(weather_data.main.temp) + "&deg;";
19
20       // set date
21
22       // convert date time to human readable
23       var date = new Date(weather_data.dt * 1000);
24
25       // update text on screen
26       document.getElementById(
27         "last-checked"
28       ).innerHTML = `Last checked: ${date.toUTCString()}`;
29
30       // main weather info
31       document.getElementById(
32         "weather-main"
33       ).innerHTML = `main: ${weather_data.weather[0].main}`;
34
35       // main weather description
36       document.getElementById(
37         "weather-description"
38       ).innerHTML = `description: ${weather_data.weather[0].description}`;
39
40       console.log(location_data); // log to console the location data
41       console.log(weather_data); // log to console the weather data
42
43       // how to drill down and display specific parts of the data
44       console.log(weather_data.weather[0].main);
45       console.log(weather_data.weather[0].description);
46
47       console.log(weather_data.dt); // get date time
48       console.log(weather_data.main.temp); // get current temp
49
50       console.log(Math.floor(weather_data.main.temp)); // round down current temp
51       console.log(date.toUTCString()); // log to console human readable
52   }
```

Function for getLocation

```
54   async function getLocation(city) {
55     var url = `http://api.openweathermap.org/geo/1.0/direct?q=${city}&limit=1&appid=fb4a8cfaa9164df205a3c8c0c0f0c8b6`;
56
57     const location = await fetch(url);
58
59     const location_data = await location.json();
60
61     return location_data;
62   }
```

Function for getWeatherData

```
64   async function getWeatherData(location_data) {
65     var lat = location_data[0].lat;
66     var lon = location_data[0].lon;
67
68     var url = `https://api.openweathermap.org/data/2.5/weather?lat=${lat}&lon=${lon}&appid=fb4a8cfaa9164df205a3c8c0c0f0c8b6&units=imperial`;
69
70     const weather = await fetch(url);
71
72     const weather_data = await weather.json();
73
74     return weather_data;
75   }
76
```

Final Project after clicking "Check Weather" button.

Tkinter Documentation

Take a few minutes to skim through the tkinter documentation. Remember how we used the api documentation for our weather app? Same thing applies here.

tkinter documentation website.

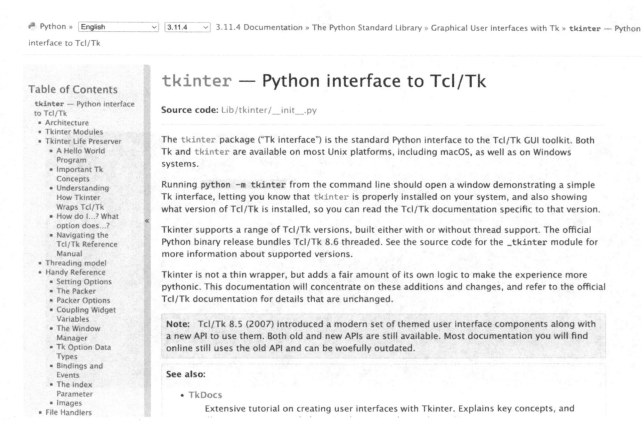

Readme file

Create a readme file for your project.

To create a readme file, just right-click in the sidebar in vscode where your file explorer is (where you see your project files). Name the file "readme.md".

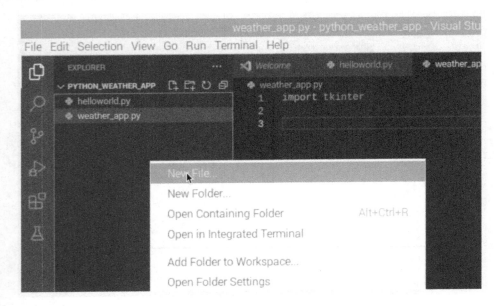

New tab opens, you can type whatever notes you want in there.

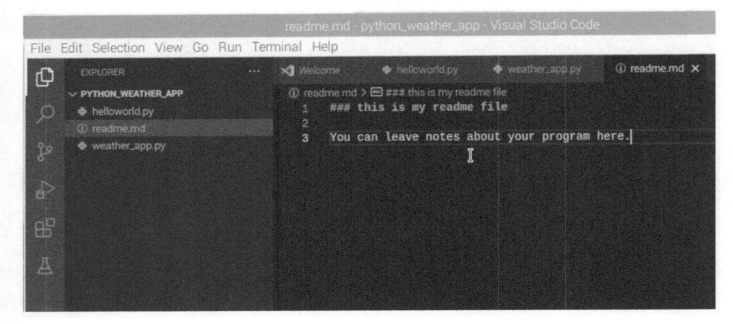

Grabbing the API key

Next, we need to go back and grab our api code from our previous app. It's located in the readme file inside of the "weather_app" folder on our desktop.

Find the folder on your desktop.

Open the folder, then open the file (right-click > open).

Copy your api code, highlight the text for all of your api key info including the URLs, then right-click > copy.

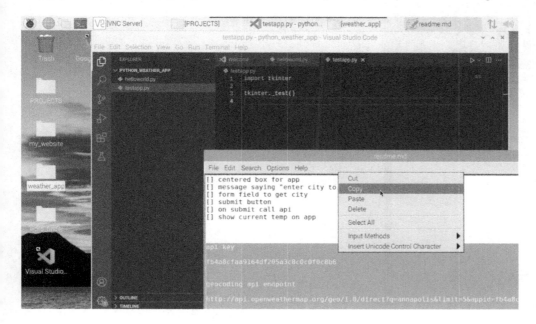

Project 2 - Python Desktop App

Now go back to vscode, then paste the api info into your readme file like so, here's how mine looks.

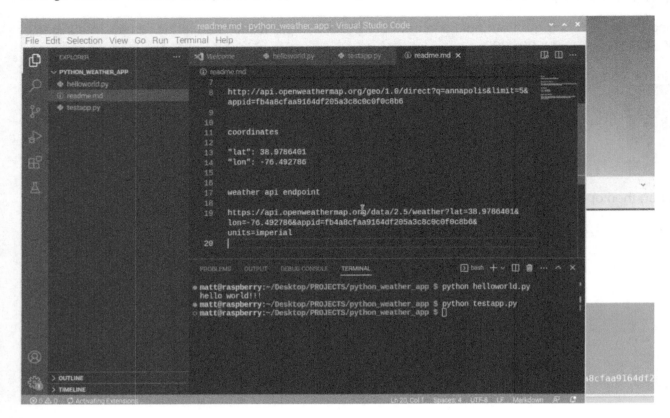

Next, go ahead and rename the file for "testapp.py" to "weather_app.py", then delete the test line.

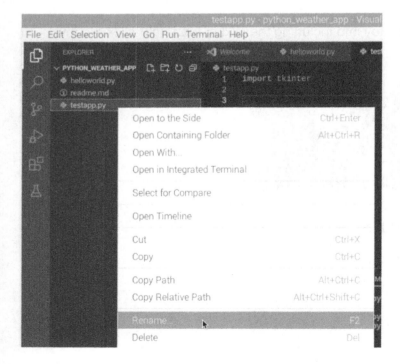

Here's how mine looks.

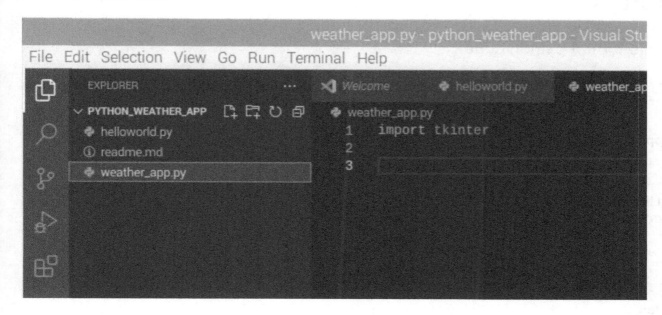

To recap - we want the weather_app.py file to have a single line of code in it:

```
import tkinter
```

If your code editor and files and code in the weather_app.py file look the same as mine, then you're ready to move on.

Here's how your app should look and work now

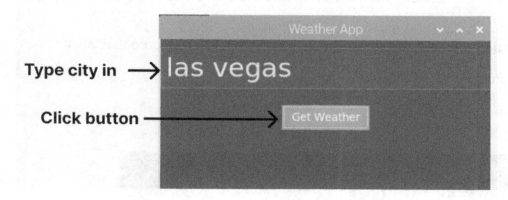

Type city in ⟶ las vegas

Click button ⟶ Get Weather

After you type the city in and click "Get Weather", a message with the city should show up in the console like this.

```
matt@raspberry:~/Desktop/PROJECTS/python_weather_app $ python weather_app.py
text from input: las vegas
```

↑
Output text to console

Updating the display

Let's take the city that we're printing to the console and instead update the window to show our output, i.e. - display the text to the window.

In order to do this we need to create a new label and then within our search function configure that label.

Put this code inside of your search function:

```
# update display to show the entry text
location_label.configure(text=f"{city}")
```

```
19          # update display to show the entry text
20          location_label.configure(text=f"{city}")
```

Then put this code where your other widgets are:

```
# city label widget
location_label = tk.Label(window, font="Roboto, 32")
location_label.pack(pady=20)
```

```
35     # city label widget
36     location_label = tk.Label(window, font="Roboto, 32")
37     location_label.pack(pady=20)
```

Here's how your app should look/work now:

We basically have everything setup now with one exception. We still need to call our api from the app.

Aside from that, all of the parts and pieces that you need to understand in order to build out the rest of this app are here.

Let's make some calls

In order to make an api call we should first think to ourselves that we need to make a function. You don't *have* to make a function but for maintainability purposes it's a good idea.

We want to give our function a city, have it call the api, then return to us that data.

Here's how we should build it.

First, we need to go to our imports and import the requests library, this will allow our program to make api calls.

Add this line to your imports:

```
import requests
```

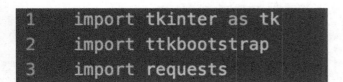

The requests library comes with python, so you don't need to install anything.

Project 2 - Python Desktop App

Next, let's create a function that uses the requests library and give it the URL string to make the api call.

We're going to use the "f sting" for the URL because both the city and the api_key are going to be variables.

```
# make request to get lat/lon from api
def location_for_city(city):
    api_url = f"http://api.openweathermap.org/geo/1.0/direct?q={city}&limit=1&appid={API_key}"
    response = requests.get(api_url)
    data = response.json()
    return data
```

Also, since the api needs a key, we can add that at the top of our code as well. Just put it right under our imports. Placing the api key at the top makes it easier to reference later. Also, we're making two api calls with this app so it will help keep our code cleaner.

```
8     # api key for weather api
9     API_key = "fb4a8cfaa9164df205a3c8c0c0f0c8b6"
```

Then all we need to do is add this one line to our code that I have highlighted here. We're printing to the console the return data from our location_for_city function that takes the city variable.

```
18   def search():
19       # get city text from frontend
20       city = city_entry.get()
21
22       # print to console the entry text
23       print(f"text from input: {city}")
24
25       # update display to show the entry text
26       location_label.configure(text=f"{city}")
27
28       # print json response from api call to console
29       print(location_for_city(city))
30
```

Here's how it should be working now

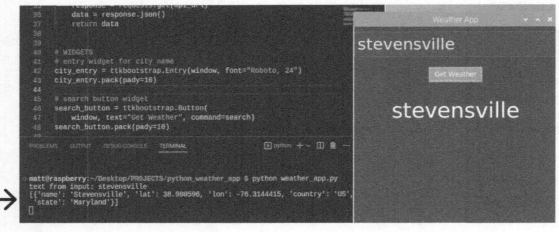

json response printed to console

352

Making a backup copy

Hover over your current file "weather_app.py" then hit Ctrl + c (copy), Ctrl + v (paste).

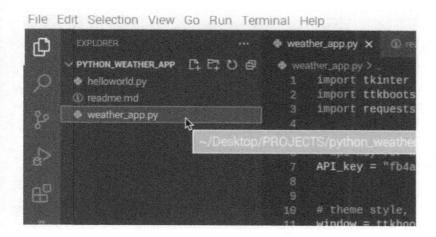

The new file should appear with the filename "weather_app copy.py"

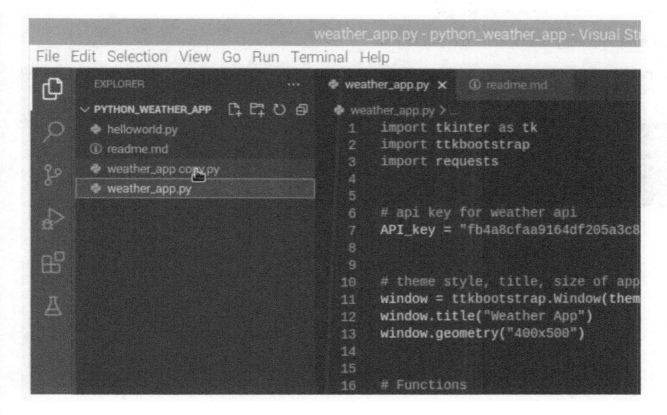

Project 2 - Python Desktop App

When the new file appears, right-click on it. Rename the file but add BACKUP at the end of it.

Now you have a backup copy of the work that you did :)

This way you can keep working on the app. Then if you completely break something, you can just copy/paste your backup code to your "weather_app.py" file and you're off to the races again.

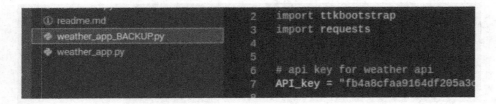

Physical challenge

Take some time to review everything that we've done together so far.

You have everything you need now to finish building this app.

If you get stuck or don't know how to do something, read the documentation, look things up, check out answers on stack overflow, do code examples on w3schools, etc.

Everything I've taught you is going to come into play now.

This is your chance to harness your "Google-Fu" skills.

Check out all the blog posts, videos and different resources available to you online. It's Python, so there's going to be A TON of support out there.

This is the best opportunity that I can give you to work on and build your ability to find your own way.

You can 100% finish this app on your own. If you get overwhelmed just pull back, think about what you are trying to do and then break the steps down.

As far as how much time this should take you?

Well… give it a couple of hours, maybe a couple of days. The thing is, you need to approach this from the perspective of just playing around, testing and breaking things. It's really the only way that you are going to learn, just have fun with it, work on one little piece at a time.

One last piece of advice – don't focus on the outcome.

Don't try to be fast, don't be in such a hurry to try to "finish" this project just so you can move onto the next thing.

Take your time to explore and play with the code. Change it, shape it, express yourself – "it's art".

You got this 💪.

Mockup

Open Figma and create a basic version of the Pomo Timer.

Building

The code for this program uses "classes" which are a part of OOP.

I picked this project because it only uses one object.

The only difference between this project and the previous ones is that you are using the word "self" a lot.

The reason you use the word "self" is because we are making the Pomodoro Timer object. All of the functions in this program are actually part of the timer.

All the code that we are writing for this program is based on describing one thing, the Pomodoro Timer, which is an object.

All the functionality is part of the Pomodoro Timer.

Learning about OOP

W3schools has a great little tutorial for you to use to get started with learning how to work with classes. I would recommend that you go ahead and take some time to play around with the code example in order to get your head around classes and objects.

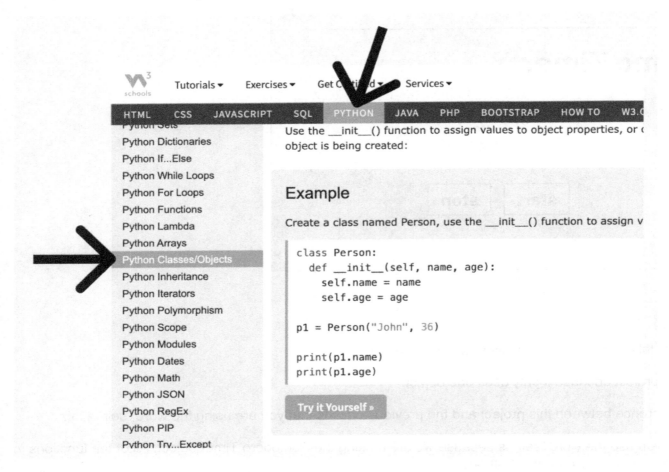

In the next section I'm going to give you the final code of the Pomo Timer. Go ahead and copy line by line the exact code that I give you. OOP is a different way of thinking about how to write code.

Take your time and just write the code out.

By the time that you finish writing the code out you should have a basic understanding of how and why you use the word "self". This is a critical first step to learning how to use OOP.

Final code

```python
1    import tkinter as tk
2    from tkinter import messagebox
3    from ttkbootstrap import ttk, Style
4
5    # set times
6    MINUTES = 60
7    WORK_TIME_SETTING = 25 * MINUTES
8    SHORT_BREAK_TIME_SETTING = 5 * MINUTES
9    LONG_BREAK_TIME_SETTING = 15 * MINUTES
10
11   # if you want to test shorter time settings
12   # WORK_TIME_SETTING = 4
13   # SHORT_BREAK_TIME_SETTING = 2
14   # LONG_BREAK_TIME_SETTING = 6
15
16
```

Project 3 - Pomodoro Timer App

```python
17    class PomodoroTimer:
18        def __init__(self):
19
20            # window settings
21            self.window = tk.Tk()
22            self.window.geometry("400x300")
23            self.window.title("Pomo Timer")
24            self.style = Style(theme="vapor")
25            self.style.theme_use()
26
27            # labels
28            self.timer_label = tk.Label(
29                self.window, text="", font=("Helvetica", 40))
30            self.timer_label.pack(pady=20)
31
32            # start timer
33            self.start_button = ttk.Button(
34                self.window, text="Start", command=self.start_timer)
35            self.start_button.pack(pady=5)
36
37            # stop timer
38            self.stop_button = ttk.Button(self.window, text="Stop", command=self.stop_timer,
39                                          state=tk.DISABLED)
40            self.stop_button.pack(pady=5)
41
42            # variables
43            self.work_time = WORK_TIME_SETTING
44            self.break_time = SHORT_BREAK_TIME_SETTING
45
46            self.is_work_time = True
47            self.pomodoros_completed = 0
48            self.is_running = False
49
50            if self.is_running:
51                print(self.pomodoros_completed)
52
53            # runs the program
54            self.window.mainloop()
55
```

```python
55
56    def start_timer(self):
57        self.start_button.config(state=tk.DISABLED)
58        self.stop_button.config(state=tk.NORMAL)
59        self.is_running = True
60        self.update_timer()
61
62    def stop_timer(self):
63        self.start_button.config(state=tk.NORMAL)
64        self.stop_button.config(state=tk.DISABLED)
65        self.is_running = False
66
```

```python
67    def update_timer(self):
68        if self.is_running:
69            if self.is_work_time:
70                self.work_time -= 1
71                if self.work_time == 0:
72                    self.is_work_time = False
73                    self.pomodoros_completed += 1
74                    self.break_time = LONG_BREAK_TIME_SETTING if self.pomodoros_completed % 4 == 0 else SHORT_BREAK_TIME_SETTING
75
76                    # pop up window alert
77                    messagebox.showinfo("Break Time" if self.pomodoros_completed % 4 == 0
78                                        else "Break Time", "Take a 30 minute break"
79                                        if self.pomodoros_completed % 4 == 0
80                                        else "Take a 5 minute break")
```

Made in the USA
Las Vegas, NV
28 December 2023

83608524R00216